The Songyang Story

PARK BOOKS

The Songyang Story

Architectural Acupuncture as Driver for Rural Revitalisation in China
Projects by Xu Tiantian, DnA_Beijing

Essays: Eduard Kögel, Saskia Sassen, Remy Sietchiping, Martino Stierli, Wang Jun and Xu Tiantian

Contents

Hans-Jürgen Commerell and Kristin Feireiss

Directors of Aedes Architecture Forum Berlin

The Story of the Story

Rural development is an area that has been globally neglected over the past 40 years, whilst the predominant focus was on the shape and growth of the cities, yet it is of existential importance for the future of communities and social cohesion. Although over half of the world's population is already living in cities, we should stress the fact that the other almost 50 per cent, still living between the metropolitan areas and the countryside, have an equal right to well-being and prosperity. Furthermore, the cities will not be able to survive without the development of rural regions. Hence, in recent years, the hinterland has become a research focus in the programme of our Aedes Architecture Forum and Campus, in exchange with our international network partners.

Our "discovery" of Songyang and its outstanding regional revitalisation programme created by the Beijing-based architect Xu Tiantian is a model we want to pass on to the world. Even if not all the methods, principles and design strategies presented in this publication are entirely applicable everywhere, the approach is exemplary.

The rural redevelopment programme Xu Tiantian has developed and realised goes far beyond the design of a few new buildings in the villages of Songyang County. Through the sensitive implementation of small-scale architectures of different functions, the architect has instigated and developed a multi-layered socio-economic healing process. These activities are starting to produce prosperity and growth that, in conjunction with larger infrastructure-connectivity projects, provide substantial incentives for people to stay in or even return to the rural region.

It is not about the size of these projects, it is about how they are designed and embedded in the rural matrix, and how the architect has interconnected them. She designed not only contemporary architecture, implemented by an acupunctural method, but also a fabric of spaces of opportunity by weaving a network of cooperatives, re-animating local, cultural craftsmanship techniques and creating a new kind of rural self-confidence and micro economy.

In 2017, we visited the region southwest of Hangzhou for the first time, aiming to explore and better understand the Songyang concept, to collect data, images and information for an exhibition in Berlin, and to produce videos of the specific sites using interviews with the local protagonists, including Songyang's magistrate Wang Jun, representing the local government, who is responsible for the application of the concept. All of this has contributed significantly to the positive reception, both in China and internationally, of our exhibition *Rural Moves – The Songyang Story* that was first shown at Aedes Architecture Forum in Berlin in March 2018 and later in Venice and Vienna.

The invitation to be a part of the official programme of the 16th International Architecture Exhibition of the 2018 Venice Biennale was an important step in attracting even more international attention from experts and the public for the Songyang Story and the importance of the "rural" topic. This momentum led to the international conference Regions on the Rise that we held in November 2018 on-site in rural China. Invited by Songyang County, we gathered together some 40 participants – including representatives from UN-Habitat – from all over the world to an experts' exchange. This networking resulted in a five-year collaboration between the government of Songyang and UN-Habitat, which was kicked off in a follow-up conference in autumn 2019.

This book is a continuation of the Songyang Story. We have added a number of new architectural projects we were not able to consider when we started our Songyang research, in particular the new typologies for social housing that Xu Tiantian implemented most recently in Songyang. This social housing programme constitutes an important step in the development of the overall endeavour and a new chapter of "The Story". Furthermore, making this publication offered the possibility to invite authors from various fields to examine the Songyang phenomenon from their perspectives, demonstrating its manifold societal, economic and ecological implications.

We are very grateful to the architect Xu Tiantian and the Songyang County People's Government for giving us a profound insight into this magnificent endeavour, and the invited authors for undertaking the journey to Songyang and contributing substantially to the story, which will continue.

Moritz Dirks and Xu Tiantian interviewing Wang Jun

Martino Stierli

The Philip Johnson Chief Curator of Architecture and Design
at The Museum of Modern Art, New York

Rural DNA

Xu Tiantian's interventionist architecture in Songyang County

China's transformation from a planned economy into a hotbed of globalisation in the early twenty-first century has been restless and breathtaking, and much ink has been spilled on this process unparalleled in human history. While this transformation has been under way for decades and has lifted dozens of millions out of poverty, creating in the process a broad and mighty middle class, the economic progress appears to be increasingly threatened by a number of gravely problematic aspects, including the persecution of ethnic minorities (in particular the Uighurs); the establishment of an increasingly perfected, oppressive surveillance state; the reckless exploitation of natural resources; and the growing gap between the urban privileged and a rural population that finds itself deprived of its traditional – agricultural and artisanal – livelihood and ways of living. As a matter of fact, the dialectic between the countryside and the metropolitan centres has for decades been heavily tilted towards rapid urbanisation, and, by consequence, a drainage of people from the countryside; a dynamic that has accelerated to such a degree that many of the Chinese megacities, foremost Beijing and Shanghai, have grown to a point where they have reached the limits of manageability, affordability, and economic and ecological sustainability more broadly. It is only in very recent years that the central government has acknowledged the threat that this acceleration towards urbanisation poses not only for the success of the Chinese model, but also for the nation's very social fabric. As a consequence, various levels of government – from local to provincial and the central government in Beijing – are increasingly turning their attention and funds towards rural communities in an effort to provide opportunities for sustainable livelihoods outside of the urban mega-centres.

In terms of architecture, China's gigantic economic and social transformation has turned the country into the largest construction site in human history,[1] with not only entire megacities built from scratch within the past two or three decades, but also an impressive investment in infrastructure. This includes the large and efficient airports, a finely woven network of reliable high-speed train services that connects not only the major population centres but also the country's hinterland, and the unprecedentedly ambitious "Belt and Road" initiative, comprising a number of transportation corridors by sea and land vaguely inspired by

1
For some key statistical data see "Read the Architecture in China by Graphs," a+u Chinese Edition 064: Architects in China (6.2016), pp. 6–7.

the ancient Silk Road, with which China asserts its economic and political ambitions on a global scale. While the vast majority of construction in the urban centres and elsewhere has been in the hands of government-run design institutes, during the massive wave of urbanisation of the 2000s the country relied on the reputation of (mainly) Western architects to put itself on the international map of architectural awareness and recognition. Indeed, it was through a select number of works (predominantly for cultural institutions such as museums, performance spaces, and the like) authored by widely known architects and firms that Chinese architecture garnered initial external interest and media exposure. Many of these architects have been given an opportunity to build on a scale and at a speed unbeknownst to them, not in all cases with equally successful results.

While China has, thus, become almost synonymous with the opportunities and pitfalls of a hyper-capitalist development, in the more recent past there has emerged a young generation of Chinese-born architects who reject this "starchitecture" paradigm. Instead, many of these individual, privately operated practices have favoured a search for a contemporary answer to the question of how modern architecture can be firmly grounded in the country's unique cultural context, without resorting to picturesque historicism or faux vernacular. In many ways, the work of these architects can be seen as a continuation of what became known in China as "experimental architecture" in the 1990s, when for the first time since the communist takeover in 1949 private architectural offices were founded outside of the state-run design institutes.[2] Many of the exponents of this generation of architects have been trained in Western universities, and through their own intermediary position between East and West have garnered some attention outside their immediate places of action by means of exhibitions, publications, lectures, teaching activities, and so on. Nevertheless, this critical research into a contemporary architecture that is both genuinely modern and Chinese continues to be overshadowed in the public perception by the heroic narratives of the giganto-maniac megaprojects of the early 2000s, at least for now.

2
For this argument see Li Xiangning, "From 'Experimental Architecture' to 'Critical Pragmatism': Practice of Contemporary Individual Architects in China," in Li Xiangning (ed.), *Contemporary Architecture in China: Toward a Critical Pragmatism* (Mulgrave, Victoria: Images Publishing, 2018), pp. 7–9.

The work of the Beijing-based architect Xu Tiantian and her DnA_Design and Architecture Studio is situated at the intersection of China's recent reappraisal of the countryside and a younger generation of architects' search for a contemporary practice grounded equally in modernity and the Chinese cultural context.[3] At the same time, Xu's extensive work in the rural Songyang County, Zhejiang Province, is unique in comparison to that of her peers in that the ultimate objective of her design work is not a singular architectural object, but rather the transformation and fortification of the local community and its economy by means of a series of small-scale architectural insertions that the architect herself calls "acupunctures".[4] Xu and her team have over the past few years collaborated closely with the local government of Songyang County, a region with a stunningly beautiful mountainous landscape situated southwest of the large population centres of Shanghai and Hangzhou. The network of literally dozens of projects that Xu has realised as a result of this collaboration include a variety of programmes and typologies: from factories and production halls intended to revive local artisanal and architectural traditions to centres of culture and community that seek to strengthen a sense of local history and identity. While in this way producing a sense of internal coherence for the inhabitants of Songyang County, the initiative also builds on the creation of a rural tourism industry geared towards the affluent population in the nearby urban centres.

3
The work of DnA and Xu Tiantian has recently been featured in an exhibition (with catalogue) at Aedes Architecture Forum, Berlin, and in a separate book publication. See Kristin Feireiss, Hans-Jürgen Commerell (eds.), DnA_Design and Architecture, *Rural Moves – The Songyang Story* (Berlin: Aedes, 2018), and Kristin Feireiss, Hans-Jürgen Commerell (eds.), DnA_Design and Architecture, *Architecture as Transformer: Projects 2004–2018* (Berlin: Aedes, 2018).

4
In architectural terminology, "acupuncture" was first introduced by Spanish architect Ignasi de Solà-Morales to describe his work in Barcelona.

Indeed, Xu Tiantian's involvement with rural China is by no means unique in the context of contemporary Chinese architecture, as evidenced in an impressive array of projects that were presented at the 16th International Architecture Exhibition of the 2018 Venice Biennale.[5] Among the works to be mentioned in this category are, to cite but a few, the renovation of Wencun village by Amateur Architecture Studio (Wang Shu and Lu Wenyu), the Bamboo Craft Village by Archi-Union Architects (Philip F. Yuan), and the Ruralation Shenaoli Library by Zhang Lei. Not all among the many similar projects for (agricultural or artisanal) production, community and cultural service, tourism, or housing are equally promising, though. In fact, several of them have unleashed or at least accelerated a counter-productive dynamic of "rural gentrification" that threatens to further marginalise the local rural populations instead of fortifying their livelihoods. Where such "renovations" of villages are not being considered with the same

5
See Li Xiangning (ed.), *Building a Future Countryside, Pavilion of China, 16th International Architecture Exhibition, La Biennale di Venezia* (New York: The Images Publishing Group, 2018)

level of care as in the instances mentioned here, these villages can easily turn into ghost towns, pretty but hollow simulacra of intact village life serving the Chinese sentiment of *xiangchou*, or nostalgia, for the (rural) homeland, which is widespread among affluent but uprooted urbanites. Or, as it has been put pointedly elsewhere, a straightforward assessment of the problems the countryside faces today and of the ways in which architecture could be employed to resolve some of these issues has suffered, among other things, from "the simplistic vision of the countryside as a dumping ground for capital and an arena for monetizing homesickness".[6] Even though the apparent initial success and appeal of Xu Tiantian's Songyang interventions may also run the risk of unleashing the spectre of mass tourism and thereby transforming the county into a sort of rural theme park, the attempt to create an alternative paradigm to urban life that provides sustainable livelihoods in the countryside is genuine and more intellectually and conceptually sophisticated here than elsewhere. As a matter of fact, and given that the economic and social rebalancing of the relationship between cities and countryside is one of the major political challenges in many countries of the developed world, Xu's work in Songyang may serve as a model from which governments and institutions in Europe and North America can learn.[7]

6
Zhang Xiaochun and Li Xiangning, "Rural Futures: Challenges and Opportunities in Contemporary China", in Li Xiangning (ed.), *Building a Future Countryside, Pavilion of China, 16th International Architecture Exhibition, La Biennale di Venezia* (New York: The Images Publishing Group, 2018), p. 5.

7
See for this point Hans-Jürgen Commerell, "The New Rural Self-Confidence in China and the Global Challenge", in Li Xiangning (ed.), *Building a Future Countryside, Pavilion of China, 16th International Architecture Exhibition, La Biennale di Venezia* (New York: The Images Publishing Group, 2018), pp. 8–11.

Xu Tiantian's buildings in Songyang

What are Xu Tiantian's buildings in Songyang about specifically? In line with a holistic approach to local traditions and dwelling patterns, her "acupunctures" are distributed across large parts of the county's territory in the form of relatively modest and unassuming structures that operate with a remarkable efficiency of means. They address a great variety of needs and programmes. *The Brown Sugar Factory* (p. 72) in Xing village serves as a place for the traditional production of an agricultural product while also providing communal space for a variety of cultural programmes for the villagers. Consisting in a prefabricated steel frame system but also using traditional materials such as bamboo for the roofing and shading of the covered corridors around the production spaces, the building acknowledges at the same time the reality of a globalised construction economy and ancient construction techniques without falling into the trap of nostalgia for the past. In its clear spatial organisation and efficiency of means, the *Brown Sugar Factory* (p. 72) is a bold statement that modernity and tradition can be brought into a meaningful conversation. Other projects, such as the *Wang Jing Memorial Hall* (p. 140) in the village of Wang or the *Hakka Indenture Museum* (p. 104), represent places of commemoration and cultural memory. The Hakka Indenture Museum in the mountain village of Shicang, in particular, is a powerful, yet respectful, insertion into the fragile village structure. Consisting of a curved, longitudinal space that is traversed by a water canal, the central space is lined with a series of side rooms for the display of documents pertaining to the history of the Hakka people who settled the mountainous regions of the county centuries ago. In this case, the architect opted for massive stone walls and local construction techniques used traditionally in houses and bridges. Her masterful use of the natural elements of light and water lend the main space a sense of solemn dignity, providing ever-changing atmospheric sensations throughout the course of the day.

Perhaps the most poetic of all of Xu's insertions is the *Bamboo Theatre* (p. 54) in a clearing in the hillside forest near Hengkeng village. Here, the architect interpreted her task to provide space for dance performances by roping up a number of bamboo trees in a circular arrangement and bending them so they would form an outdoor dome. The project is radical both in its power of reminding us that the demarcation of a space is a fundamental act of architecture, and in its proposal that architecture entirely made of renewable natural resources may be conceivable; and thus, an idea of architecture that is not fundamentally separated from the natural environment, but an organic part of it. If we follow Bruno Latour's observation that a new paradigm is needed between the two poles of the (progressive) global and the (reactionary) local that is firmly grounded in the understanding of the limited resources of our planet, then Xu Tiantian's *Bamboo Theatre* may serve as an example of what such an architecture of the "terrestrial" may look like.[8]

8 See Bruno Latour, *Down to Earth: Politics in the New Climatic Regime* (Cambridge: Polity Press, 2018).

Xu Tiantian

Architect, DnA_Design and Architecture, Beijing

Architectural Acupuncture

For centuries, China had been an agrarian society with a demographic distribution weighted heavily towards rural areas and an economy that primarily relied on agriculture. Once the economic reform was launched in the early 1980s, the rural population began to pour into cities seeking opportunities to earn a better living. This momentum resulted in half the Chinese population living in cities, causing a fundamental transformation in the state's economic structure. As the majority of the labour force shifted from rural areas to the cities, the countryside was left with the elderly and the children of the labour force, unattended farmland, vacant and run-down houses, and the agrarian cultures and traditions from past centuries. Songyang County, part of Lishui City, in the southwestern part of Zhejiang Province, was not exempt from this situation. In 2014, the county consisted of more than 400 villages in an area spanning over 1,406 square kilometres with a total population of 240,000. Its rural to urban demographic ratio is roughly 4:1. Underneath Songyang's idyllic and picturesque sceneries where clusters of ancient villages are strung along rolling hills with tea bushes on their slopes, lies an unbalanced demography and dormant economy.

To address this loss of the labour force and revive the countryside, the Songyang County People's Government launched a rural development initiative six years ago. This is where our collaboration began. Our first projects revolved around the Damushan Tea Plantation and some of the villages, including the *Pingtian Village Centre* (p. 60), the Damushan *Teahouse* (p. 36), and the *Bamboo Pavilion* (p. 46) among many others. All of these projects have become learning processes for us to understand local construction materials and techniques, as well as an exchange of ideas that renewed the locals' preconceptions about construction. We learned bamboo construction from Xu Chaoran, our contractor and an expert on bamboo structure. Through the Hengkeng villagers we discovered a way to transform a creek into a water terrace using the minimum amount of stone and cement. However, we also had to overcome many obstacles – with the construction in Pingtian, for example. Here we worked with Mr. Wu, a local expert on the conservation of buildings such as ancestor's halls. He did not see the value of renovating the cluster of buildings that later became the *Pingtian Village Centre* (p. 60). It was only by the end of the project, when Mr. Wu told me that he would like to build a house like this one in his home village, that I finally realised our concept had fully convinced him.

The experiences we had with these early projects helped us both to understand the issues we needed to address through architectural intervention and to realise the dormant potentials in the natural and cultural capitals of Songyang. We began to contemplate a strategy that would not only temporarily alleviate the symptoms of the issue, but also improve the system holistically. Acupuncture, a practice in traditional Chinese medicine, shares a similar conceptual notion with what we needed to achieve. By pinpointing the needles on a set of meridian points on the human body, according to the functions of various systems of the organs, the interaction of these networks of interventions results in improving the well-being of one's overall health rather than only targeting the symptoms.

We proposed "architectural acupuncture" as a systematic and sustainable rural strategy for Songyang County to regain its "rural self-confidence". By adopting an approach of minimal interventions, multifunctional public programmes are introduced to different villages and rural regions, each tailored to the complexity of the respective cultural heritage and context. Applied with vernacular materials and construction techniques, architectural acupuncture integrates nature back into the villages, thus restoring their rural identity, whilst stimulating local economic development. Similar to the way acupuncture releases trapped energy at various meridian points on the body to restore the overall health of a person, architectural acupuncture is a strategy aimed at motivating and inspiring villages and communities to initiate their own self-regeneration for further development. Moreover, the concept of architectural acupuncture aims to activate the dormant resources and generate circulation among the villages in Songyang by establishing links with the nearby regions and beyond.

The rich Hakka culture and indenture heritage of Shicang village stood out as one of the first acupuncture projects. The Hakkas, meaning "the guest people", escaping from war, settled in

Shicang over 200 years ago. The Hakka Indenture collection there – the largest in the country – is an important archive for Chinese Hakka culture. The name of the village can be translated as "stone cave", which refers to a cautionary tale. To commemorate the heritage that ultimately identifies this community, the *Hakka Indenture Museum* (p. 104) is programmed as a public space built from local stones while adopting traditional techniques. This museum was as much an opportunity to restore the heritage of local construction – a process whereby three masonry experts passed on their skills to a dozen young workers – as it was an attraction for investment to convert vacant farmhouses in adjacent villages into homestays, and other new touristic programmes. The number of tourists to the village has increased from 1,000 to 5,000 per month in two years.

In the case of Xing village, brown sugar, a local product, became the stimulator that connected the economy of its vicinity. Unlike other traditional villages, Xing has maintained a rather steady population and its agricultural production generates sufficient income for villagers to build new modern houses. So brown sugar production became the key element for introducing the village's heritage. The traditional cooking process is a fascinating operation, but the family workshops were in poor condition. This new factory was programmed to engage family workshops by improving their production conditions. This multifunctional building, designed for both production and public education, has elevated the price of sugar and the villagers' income. Consequently, 50 former villagers settled back in their hometown, and 12 young villagers joined the sugar production union. The total number of tourists per annum increased from 200 in 2016 to 15,000 in 2019. In other words, this local product became a catalyst for other tourism programmes initiated by the Xing villagers. The old Wang village was located within a zoned industrial area for many years, surrounded by modern factories. In spite of its dire economic status, the pride of the villagers when they talked about their ancestor Wang Jing impressed us profoundly. This inspired a *Wang Jing Memorial Hall* (p. 140) in the centre of the village. Together with the conversion of the *Shimen Bridge* (p. 128) nearby, the area congregated into a network of tourist sites that, in turn, generated all kinds of business opportunities ranging from small shops to the villagers' engagement in restoring their ancestor's halls and ancient roads. On the opening day of the Wang Jing Memorial Hall, hundreds of villagers dressed up for the memorial ceremony. Since the completion of this project in early 2018, more than 30 villagers have set up new small tourism businesses, with over 300,000 RMB annual income in total.

Caizhai is a traditional mountain village that has been built along a river over the past 200 years. The village is best known for its tofu production in the county region, but the products from the traditional family workshops did not meet the current standard for industrially certified food. A new *Tofu Factory* (p. 194) was programmed, on a linear slope following the topography of its location, to upgrade traditional tofu production. This will allow the tofu products to be sold in city supermarkets, thus increasing the village's economic revenue. Serving as a site for both production and exhibition, its covered walkway is a leisure space where visitors and villagers can observe the tofu production process in sequence. A village union has been set up to operate the factory, engaging family workshops as shareholders of this collective economic entity.

Acupuncture cultivates architecture into a multi-dimensional expression that generates new experiments and explorations for the place and the people. Each building is holistically integrated into nature, the village and the community. It embodies the village's heritage and identity through an architectural design that restores village pride and attracts tourism. Hence, the complexity in the notion of "architecture as acupuncture" is also carried out as a social structure. Unlike some touristic villages in the country, which have had massive amounts of investment, the Songyang acupuncture strategy works within a limited budget to motivate and inspire local communities as well as attract external investments and resources.

Soon after we completed these initial projects, more and more villages expressed interest in joining the acupunctural system. Some even came up with detailed programme proposals. For example, the papermaking factory in Dalinggen village was initiated by the community only after thorough research and discussion within the village had been conducted. Eventually, the factories and workshops will build up a new economic circulation within the whole county. For example, the pottery factory will provide packaging products for rice wine and brown sugar, and the silk farming factory and papermaking factory will provide dyeing material for the workshop in the *Pingtian Village Centre* (p. 60). Each factory has a union set up for the villagers to operate it, run by family workshops as the shareholders of this collective economic entity. In fact, all of the acupuncture projects have become triggers inspiring further initiatives invested in by either the communities themselves or private investors. This has generated a new model for the rural economy that integrates cultural heritage, traditional production and rural tourism.

The housing situation in rural villages is often the opposite of that of urban locations. Most houses in rural areas are vacant; many have been abandoned for years owing to the decreased population. Shangtian village, whose history can be traced back 600 years, was becoming a "hollow village" with only a few families left. Unlike the other homestay businesses in the county that are invested in by urban private sectors, for this project we reached common agreements with the local community and government to establish a co-op system owned and financed by the village community and local government. Villagers became shareholders with their properties serving as assets. The remaining villagers are employed by tourism-related businesses. This experimental co-op system preserves the ownership and village's potential value, while avoiding rip-offs or the inequality created by external urban investments.

Acupuncture stimulations expanded beyond the villages to the vast rural region in areas such as infrastructure facilities and tourism facilities in scenic districts. Dushan Mountain, a gateway to Songyang, is the most important iconic landmark in the county. Programming a visitor centre and water sports facilities will make this project the first meeting point of local people and visitors. The *Water Conservancy Centre* (p. 206) repurposes the county's conservancy management facilities into a site for a cultural education programme for the public. Subsequently, the location and function of these projects provide a platform for connection and interaction between the urban and rural areas.

The process of revitalisation is intended neither to isolate rural areas from their urban counterparts nor to convert any rural area into an urban expression. Rather, its goal is to activate the interactions between them by restoring a rural identity. As living conditions in the villages improve, the younger generation of the labour force are motivated to return to their homes. In addition, the pleasant environment and accommodations can also attract urban residents to visit or even relocate to village living. Facilitated by the internet and modern infrastructure, the rural can provide an alternative mode of living to the urban. The acupuncture strategy is not targeted at local symptoms, but aims to bring interaction between rural and urban areas. For example, the tea education programmes and the innovative tea products generated at Damushan *Teahouse* (p. 36) have become a popular cultural tourism project and attracted thousands of students from many cities over the last year. A new start-up in Pingtian village, initiated by Ye Ke and Liu Yuli who returned home from Hangzhou city, brought new e-commerce opportunities to this ancient village. Hence, the strategy of architectural acupuncture is adopted to establish a linkage between the rural and the urban, and its stimulation of critical areas aims to generate an equilibrium between the two, as well as the well-being of the overall system.

Since our initial projects in Songyang, the area has witnessed a significant increase in population growth, tourism and tourism-related business, all of which have translated into an increase in revenue. The gross revenue from tourism in Songyang County increased from 8.4 million RMB in 2014 to 41.9 million RMB in 2018. The number of returnees from cities reached 6,000 in 2019. Most of them initiate or participate in the rural tourism programmes with their education and experience from the cities.

On 30th May, 2019, UN-Habitat, during its first UN-Habitat Assembly, announced the Songyang Innovative Rural Development Programme (Songyang Programme), a collaboration with the Songyang County People's Government, China. "Architectural acupuncture" has been adopted by UN-Habitat as an "Inspiring Practice on Urban-Rural Linkages". We hope that our Songyang Story will provide a sustainable stimulus model both in concept and in practice that can benefit other rural regions.

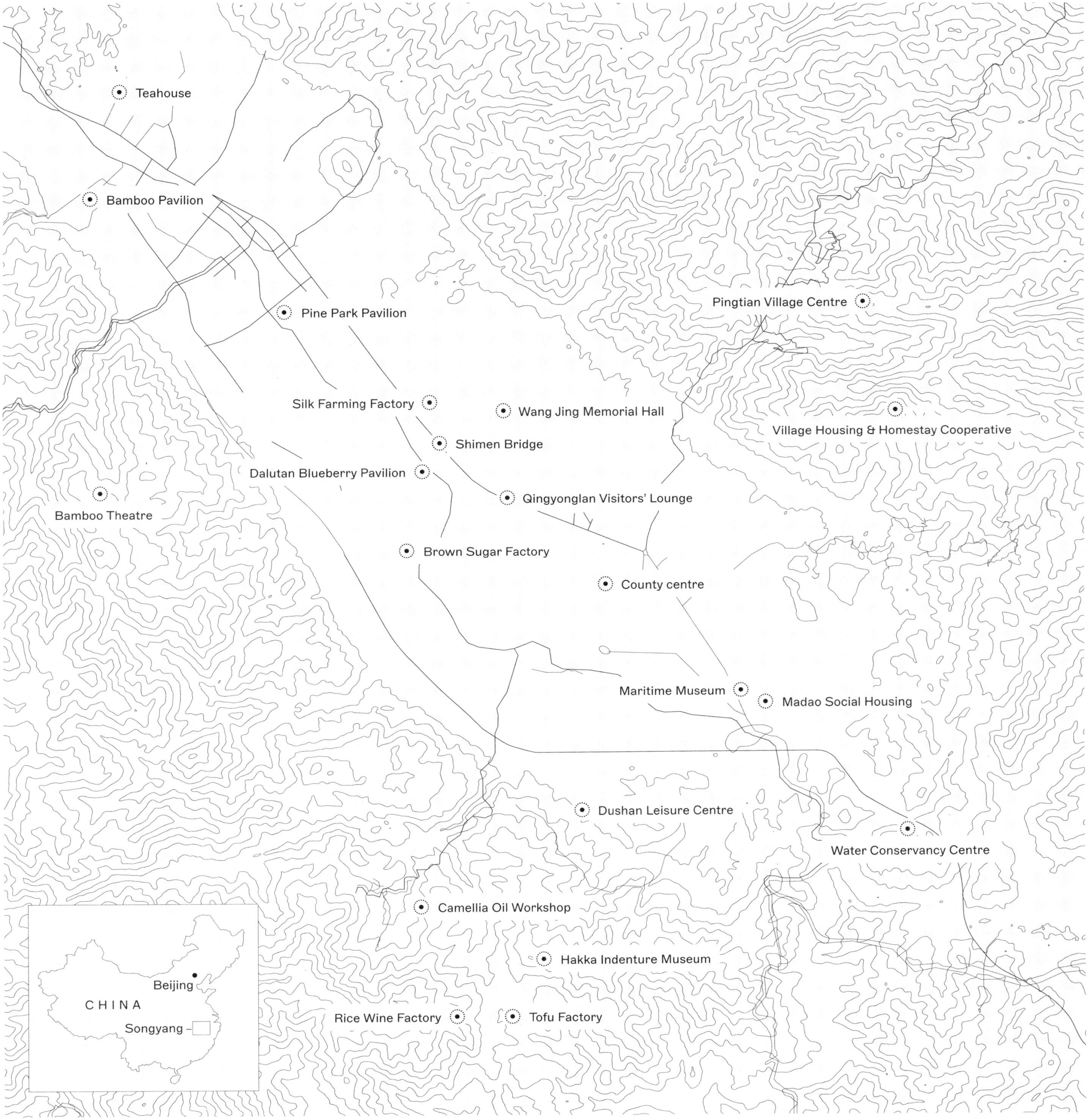

Projects in the Songyang region

Eduard Kögel

Freelance Author, Curator of the internet platform chinese-architects.com, Research Consultant and Program Curator for ANCB The Aedes Metropolitan Laboratory Berlin, Member of the Board of stadtkultur international e.V.

Rural Development through the Lens of Architecture

Triggered by serious problems of demographic and economic development in rural areas, architects and politicians are looking for new solutions.

Rural culture shaped China until the end of the twentieth century. The garden and agriculture were constituent elements of society. From 1949 until the end of the Cultural Revolution in 1976, the communist party was based in the countryside. Then the enormous urbanisation started, washing the rural population into the cities within a few years, where they lived as migrant workers with limited residence rights. Architects and planners concentrated on the emerging urban sector, which demanded a lot of resources. Rural China was out of focus, and this neglect accelerated migration.[1] In particular, the young and well-educated left their villages to seek their fortunes in the city. Old people and children remained and were unable to cope with the situation on their own.

1
According to official statistics, Lishui City which belongs to Songyang County, lost about five per cent of its population between 2005 and 2015.

How must the rural economy be shaped today so that local people can make a good living? In recent years, they have no longer been able to live from subsistence farming, which is why new approaches are needed. The potential of whole regions needs to be reviewed to support the creation of new income opportunities. However, here lies one of the major challenges: the regions in China differ widely in terms of both their natural resources and their current economic base. The digital revolution has opened up a new field for the distribution of locally produced goods, which must, however, meet the needs of consumers. What could be more appropriate than a small-scale approach that can take account of local specificities in the context of new major infrastructures such as the internet?

To address these issues, Aedes organised an exhibition entitled *Rural Moves*, which was first shown at Aedes Architecture Forum in Berlin in 2018.[2] The example of architect Xu Tiantian's projects in Songyang enabled us to present new developments and pose questions that are relevant both in China and in the West. In many countries, rural development has been neglected for many years, while the pressing problems of the metropolises claimed all resources. So it is not only about economic development, but also about a cultural commitment

2
The exhibition was curated by Hans-Jürgen Commerell and the author. Two Aedes catalogues were published: DnA_Design and Architecture, *Rural Moves – The Songyang Story*, (Berlin: Aedes, 2018), and DnA_ Design and Architecture, *Architecture as Transformer: Projects 2004–2018* (Berlin: Aedes, 2018).

promoting authentic self-esteem. The projects by Xu Tiantian presented in this publication show only a part of the developments actually taking place in Songyang and do not claim to be easily transferable to other regions. It is mainly the strategy described by the architect as "acupuncture" that can be useful for other rural areas. However, the selected examples are intended to raise curiosity about development in rural areas, which might effectuate great things on a small scale, not only in China.

Parts of the exhibition *Rural Moves* were shown in the Arsenale at the Venice Biennale of Architecture later in 2018, and the entire exhibition was presented at the Az W Architekturzentrum Vienna in the spring of 2019. At the same Biennale in 2018, the Chinese pavilion curated by Li Xiangning also had the theme "Building a Future Countryside". The Taiwanese pavilion dealt with architecture in rural areas too, with an exhibition titled *Living with Sky, Water & Mountain. Making Place in Yilan*, which showed the approach of FieldOffice Architects.[3] The high level of interest and the resulting debate show that there are attractive conditions for architectural interventions in rural areas.

3
Exhibition catalogue: *Living with Sky, Water & Mountain. Making Place in Yilan* (Taichung: National Taiwan Museum of Fine Arts, 2018).

New rural architecture in Songyang

Contrary to the local stakeholders' initial impulse to follow metropolitan examples, Xu Tiantian and her firm, DnA_Design and Architecture, focused from the very beginning on locally available resources and craft traditions that have frequently been forgotten. Traditional know-how is consequently preserved and handed down from one generation to the other through use. The ideas of a village population, however, often deviate at first from the goals of the architect and many discussions and negotiations are needed to familiarise the population with the architecturally envisioned objectives. Their experience with rammed earth buildings, for example, whose roofs have been leaking for years and whose sanitary installations have been neglected for decades, does not make them confident regarding the renewal of existing buildings or the reutilising of traditional technologies today. Therefore, the upgrading of rammed earth buildings in the village of Pingtian to create a community centre required a lot of persuasion by Xu Tiantian, since the construction foreman had very different ideas. However, following arduous negotiations and once the construction work had been completed, he did embrace the ideas, which today help him to employ similar concepts in his day-to-day practice. The aesthetic dimension and the concept of integration within existing buildings are attractive for visitors, because they promote an authentic culture. Here, a cycle is created in which a position becomes established based on constructive discussions, thus uniting local pride and expectations for the future in a holistic overall appearance.

The more the population recognises this special quality as being attractive for visitors from the city, the easier it will be for architects to advocate upgrading rural culture based upon it. *Rural Moves* in Songyang showed that many aspects have to be taken into account and that it is important not only to position the strategies in a local context, but also to seek out a global discourse, through which the results can provide an impulse for change. Xu Tiantian's projects have ample potential in this regard.

Teahouse

Damushan Area 2015

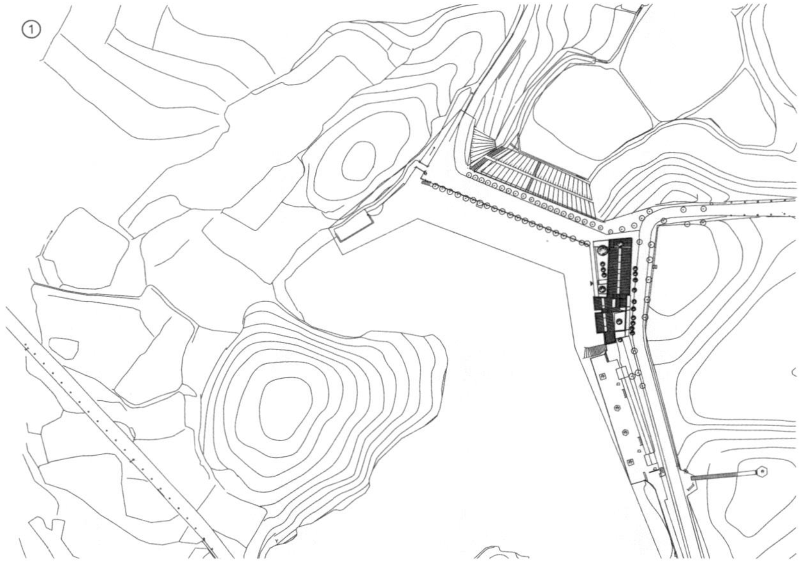

Client: Songyang County Tourism Development Cooperation Limited

The tea plantations in the Damushan area of Songyang are situated in a hilly landscape against a backdrop of imposing mountains. They extend over the ridges of the hills in smooth sweeps and have shaped the landscape with their linearly planted tea bushes for centuries.

A pond constructed between the tea plantations for irrigation in 1968 was surrounded by a path for pedestrians and cyclists. At the edge of this pond Xu Tiantian designed a teahouse for visitors affording a view of the charming scenery. The new building was embedded in such a way that it was possible to preserve five large sycamore trees, which shade the forecourt with their leafy canopy. The tea pavilion, made of black-dyed concrete, consists of a series of different spaces. The two-storey, open main room has a skylight and a glass front towards the pond. Here visitors can experience the traditional Chinese tea culture, and experts can attend workshops to obtain tea ceremony certificates. Connected to the main room are further spaces for private tea ceremonies, followed by a meditation room with a round opening through which the sunlight, reflected by the surface of the water, enlivens the interior space. Small courtyards interrupt the sequence of spaces.

① Site plan
② Axonometric drawing
1 meditation; 2 tea room; 3 courtyard; 4 rest room; 5 reception area; 6 outdoor passageway; 7 office
③+④ Section
⑤ Front elevation

②

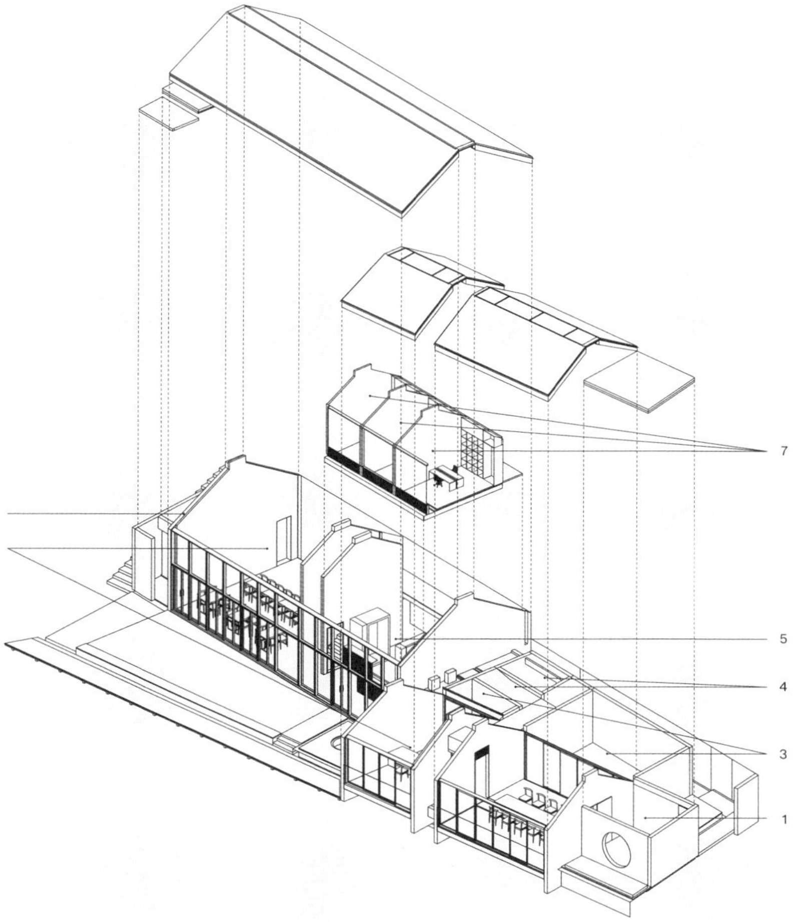

③

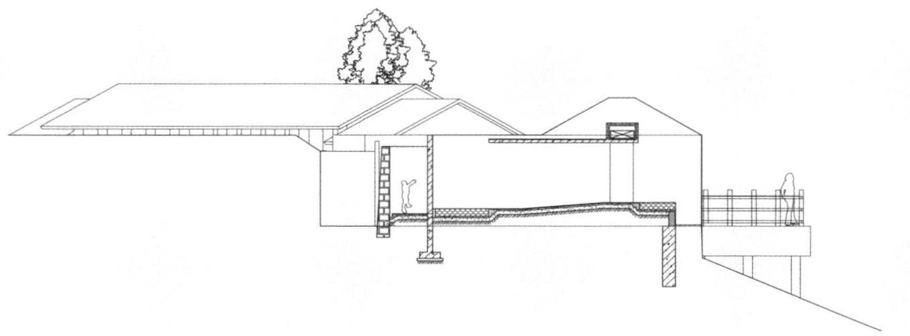

④

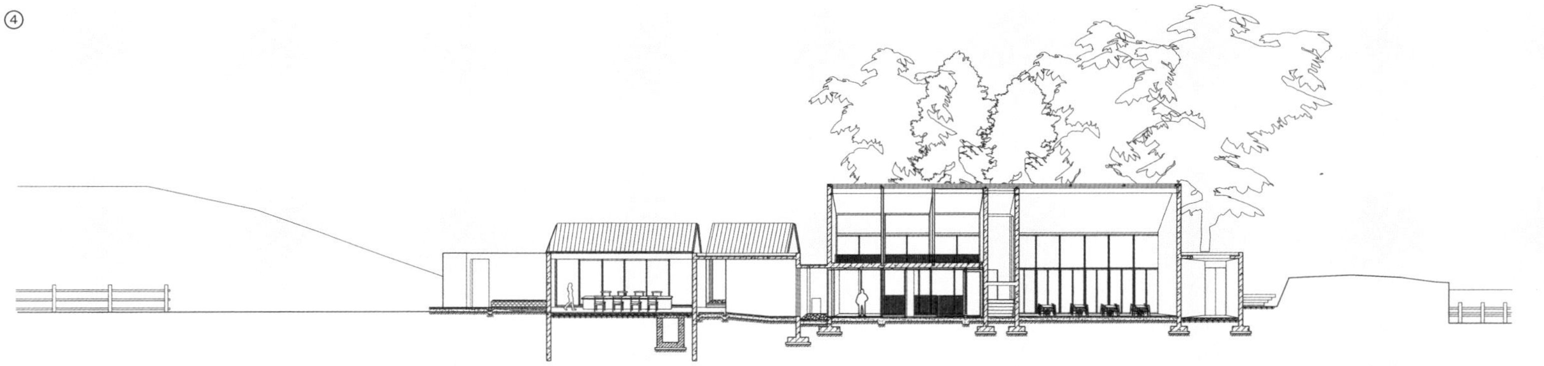

⑤

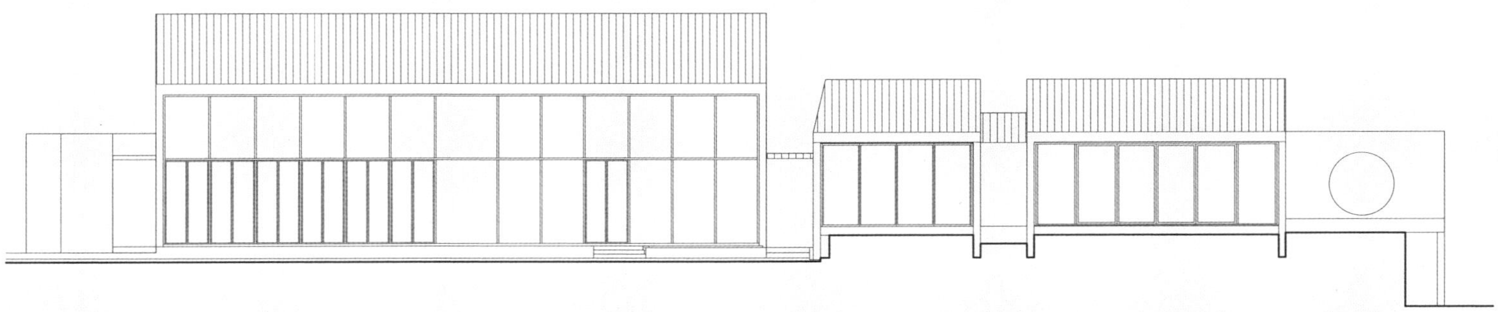

Bamboo Pavilion

Damushan Area 2015

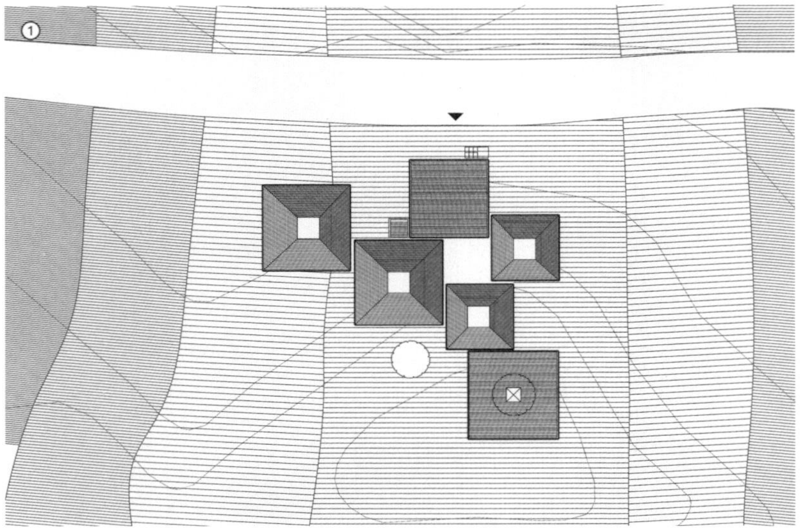

Between the tea fields of the Damushan area run narrow, paved paths providing access to the plantations and serving as infrastructure for locals and tourists. Visitors can glide through the elegantly rolling landscape using electric vehicles or bicycles or on foot and enjoy the view of the surroundings at selected locations. For a number of new viewing platforms Xu Tiantian developed a system of pavilions – consisting of a simple bamboo structure – that are positioned additively, in various sizes, on the periphery of the tea plantations. With allusions to the local traditional slanted roofs, the groups of buildings call to mind the silhouettes of historical hamlets in an abstract way. As focal points in the vast green expanses of the tea fields, the transparent structures provide a framework that is also used for temporary cultural events. By drawing a new picture of the tea plantation landscape, this, Xu Tiantian's first commission, became an important vehicle for promoting the renewal of the area.

Client: Songyang County Tourism Development Cooperation Limited

① Site plan
② Axonometric drawing
1 ribbed grid, gaps of 5mm, phyllostachys praecox; 2 load bearing structure, density reduces from outwards inside; 3 supporting structure; 4 platform
③ Sectional perspective
④ Section

③

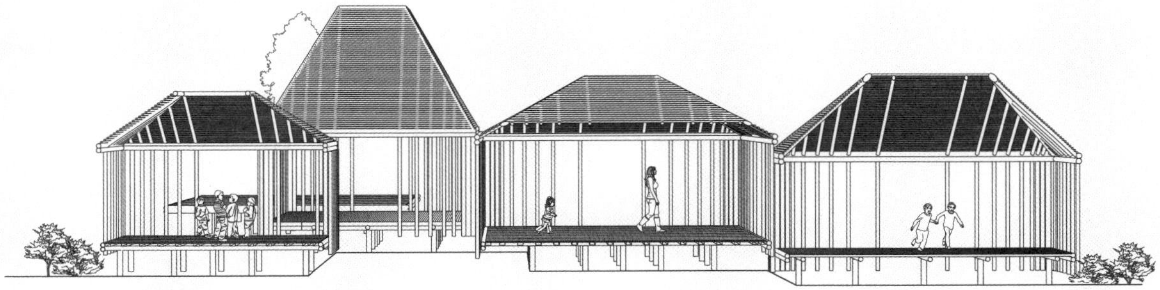

④

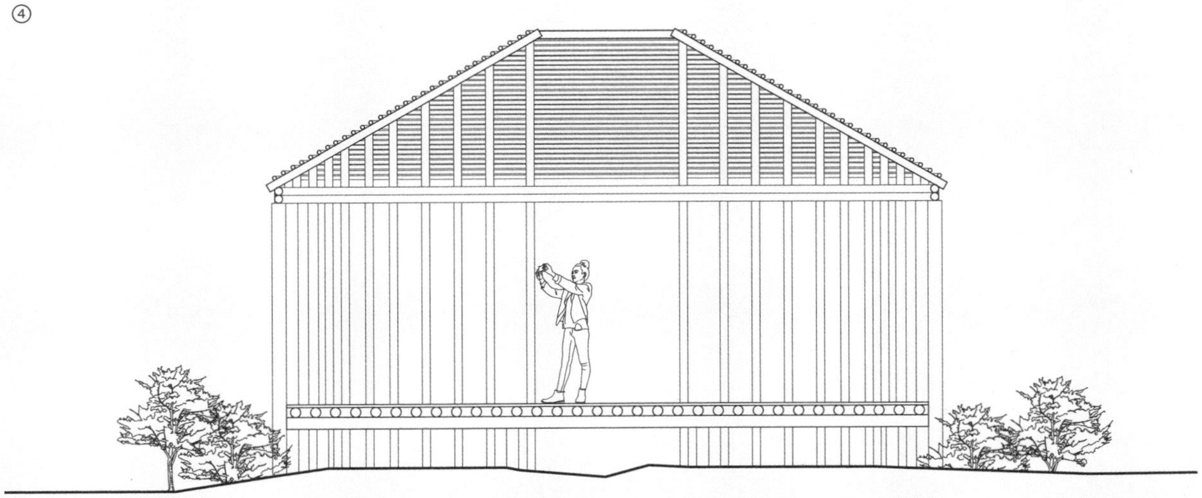

②

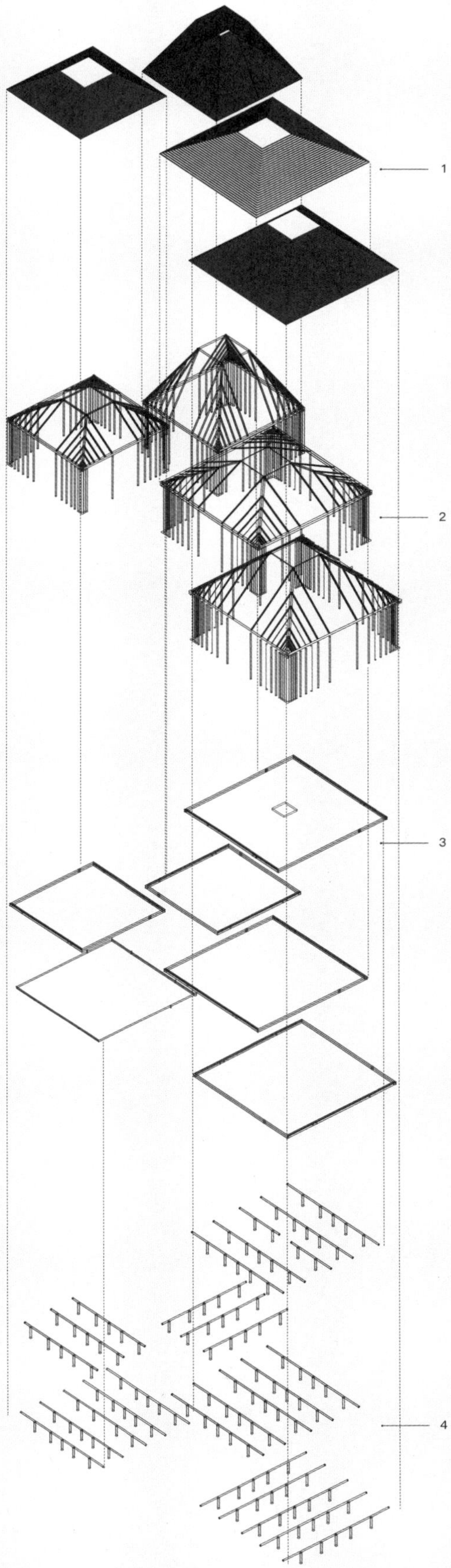

Bamboo Theatre

Hengkeng Village 2015

In the sixteenth century, the painter Qiu Ying drew a scroll of the garden of the eleventh-century historian Sima Guang in Luoyang, which was named *Garden of Solitary Enjoyment*. One section of the scroll shows a studio for planting bamboo. Inspired by this depiction of a circular ring of bamboo plants tied together on top to form a dome, Xu Tiantian designed a theatre stage in a bamboo grove in Hengkeng village.

The bamboo plant can be bent and still grows – and as soon as it is released, it will spring back powerfully into its original position. In ancient times, this constitution was understood as a reference to disagreeable officials, who after some time returned to their former position.

For the bamboo theatre, the plants were bent in a certain pattern and woven into a vault with a circular opening at the top. The growing dome needs little maintenance and the villagers only have to remove old poles annually and weave young bamboo shoots into the existing frame. This cultivation adds an extraordinary outdoor space in which village activities can be held. An irregular flowing platform made of bamboo poles in the centre allows the space to be used for performances, but also for meditation in nature. This combination of historic literati tradition with simple, local know-how beautifies the village and transforms the idyllic landscape into a contemporary place that also attracts tourists.

Client: Songyang County Tourism Development Cooperation Limited

① Extract from Qiu Ying, *Garden of Solitary Enjoyment* (1515–52), © John L. Severance Fund 1978.67.
②–④ Diagram of the construction process
⑤ Section

②

③

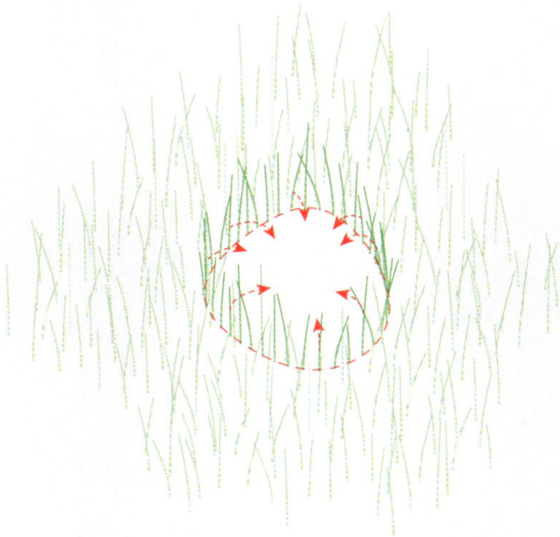

④

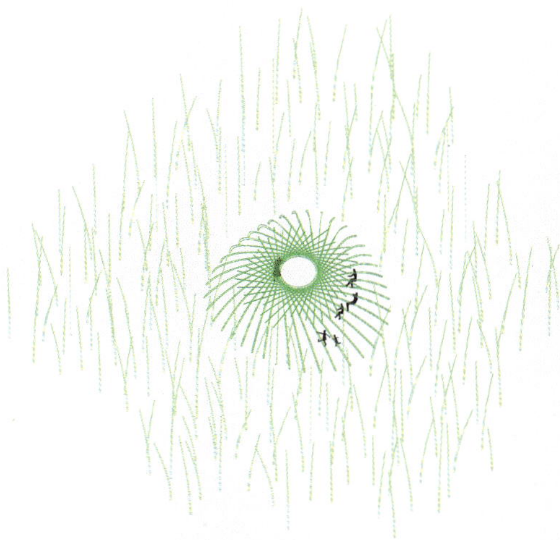

⑤

Pingtian Village Centre

Pingtian Village 2015

The village of Pingtian is situated on a mountain ridge and its houses consist mainly of rammed earth walls with traditional wood constructions supporting the roofs. The houses are grouped organically within the topography and can be accessed on foot via stairs and very narrow alleyways.

For an exhibition space dedicated to traditional agricultural equipment and a handcraft centre, the architect Xu Tiantian decided not to tear down the existing structures, but repair parts of one group of buildings and re-organise others so that the old building fabric met contemporary requirements. The L-shaped exhibition spaces for agricultural equipment on the bottom level can be accessed from two sides. The upper level can be entered from a higher-lying alley at the back, and is also connected with the next building, which young designers use as a workshop for indigo dye. The workshop building was created from two identical houses standing close together, which are now connected by means of a newly installed skylight. Two units with outstanding views, which are available for rent, were created on the top floor.

The handling of existing structures was new for the local craftspeople and provoked resistance that had to be overcome though arduous discussions. The craftspeople wanted new materials and new forms of expression, which, however, had already led to the destruction of the historically developed culture of form and material. In the case of this example in Pingtian, the architect succeeded in persuading the local population that, by using local means, it is possible to come up with a contemporary solution that takes their needs into account while preserving the identity of the village. As a result, many locals have since taken the initiative to renovate their own buildings.

Client: People's Government of Sidu Village in Songyang County

① Site plan
② Axonometric drawing workshop studio
③ Sectional perspective exhibition hall
④ Axonometric drawing exhibition hall

③

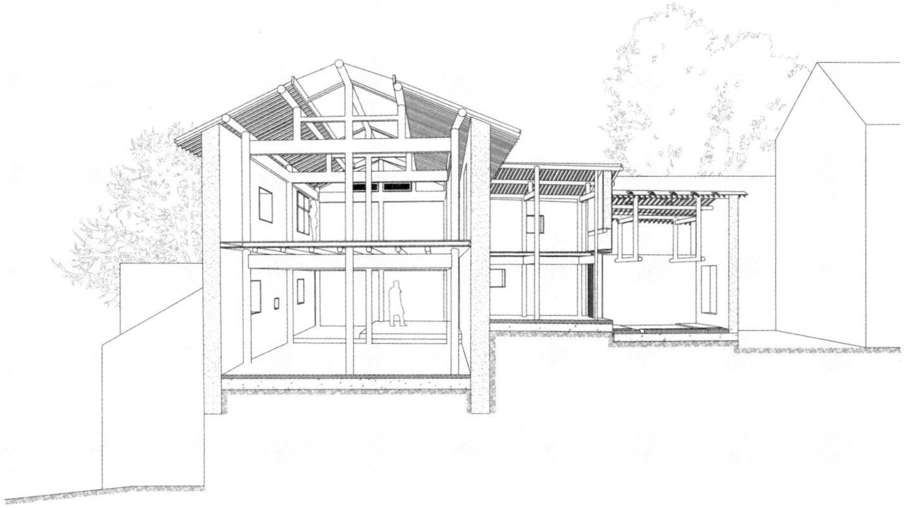

④

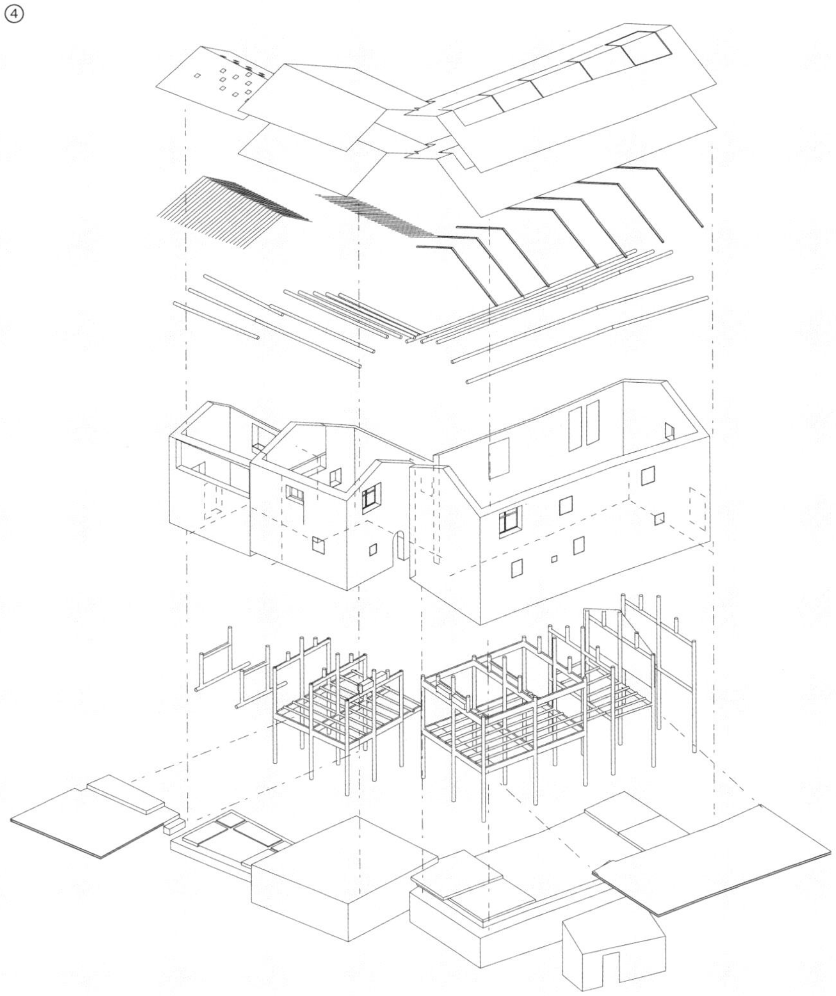

②

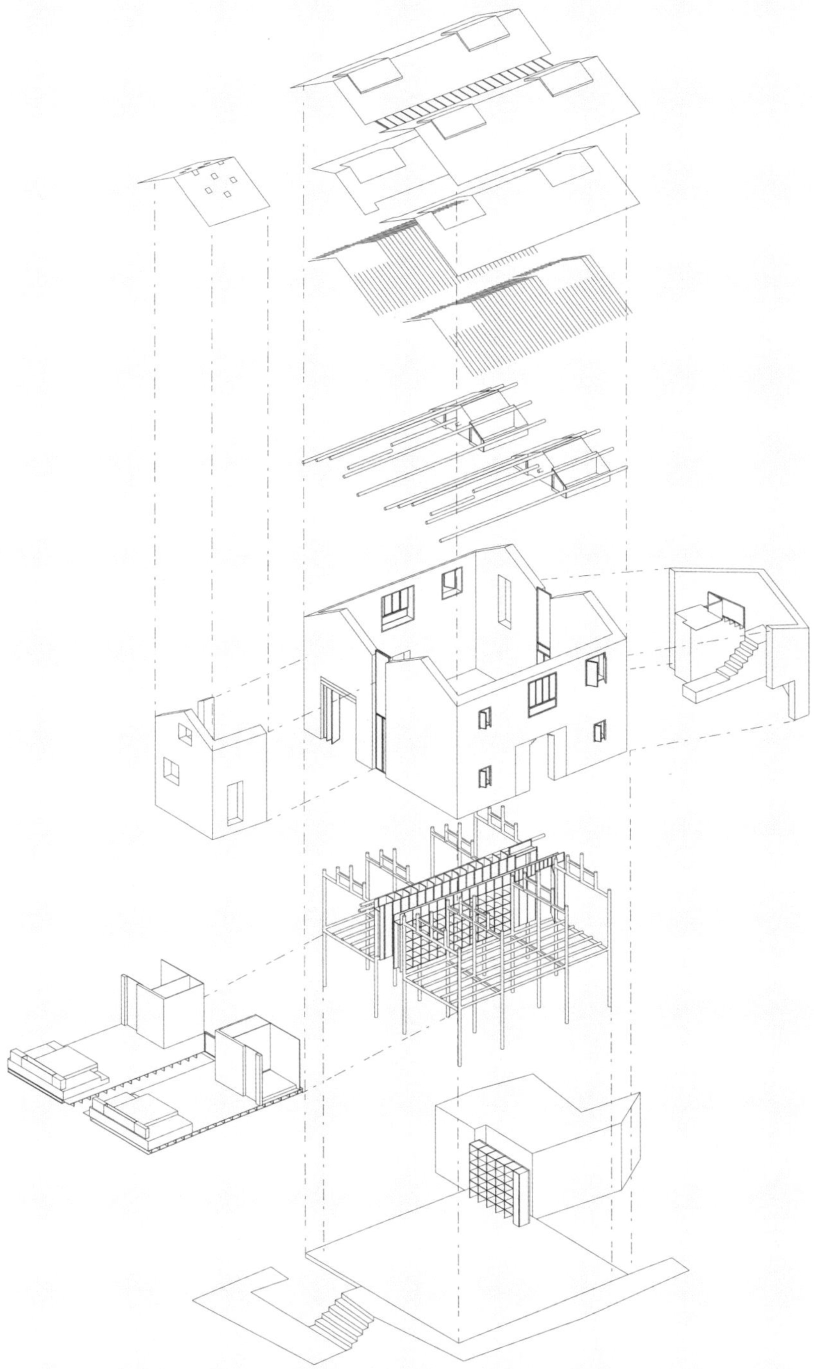

Brown Sugar Factory

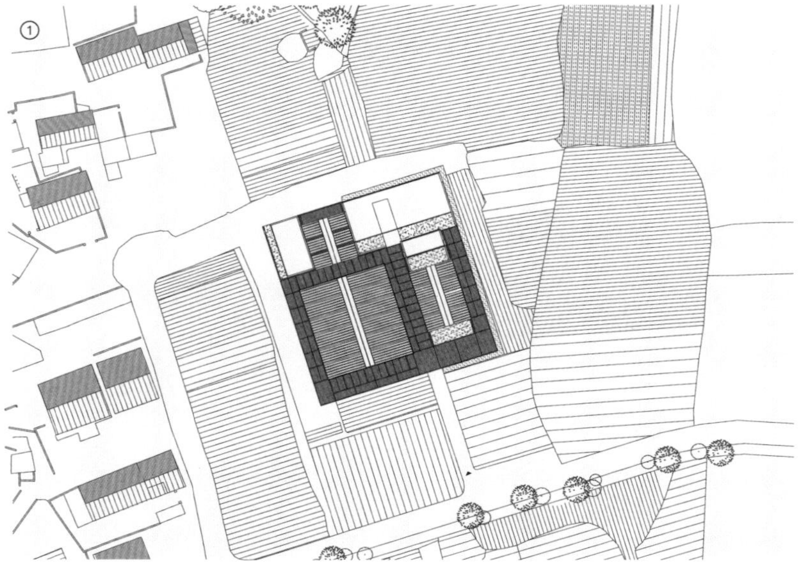

Xing Village 2016

The village of Xing is located close to the Songyin River. The region is important for the cultivation of sugar cane and the production of brown sugar, which is now the village's primary source of income. Before, the villagers produced the sugar in big iron pots in their own courtyards but had no licence to officially sell their product. The new factory has now made this possible.

Located on the edge of the village, the new factory/community building consists of several elements accommodating various functions and connected to each other by corridors. The completely transparent ground floor links the work zones to the adjacent fields and the neighbouring village structure. However, the main room with the ovens is only actively used for sugar production in the three winter months between October and December. It was therefore important to design the building in such a way that the village community can use it for other activities during the day for tea, while in the evening films are screened or the local puppet theatre gives performances.

The transparency between the different building elements and the unobstructed view of the processes involved in the production of brown sugar also make the building attractive for visitors. The reduced materiality of bricks, steel construction, glass and corrugated sheet metal creates a workroom that takes the cultural concerns of the village community into consideration. With a space for contemporary production and a meeting place for social life and culture, the architecture shapes the community as well as the economic progress in the village in a sustainable way.

Client: People's Government of Xing Village in Songyang County

① Site plan
② Axonometric drawing for structure and material
1 roof system; 2 truss frame; 3 hollow brick & curtain walls
③ Detail
1 laminated glass on steel profile; 2 porch with bamboo shading; 3 polished concrete floor; 4 gutter; 5 gravel; 6 indoor garden; 7 polished concrete floor; 8 glazed facade
④+⑤ Sectional perspective

②

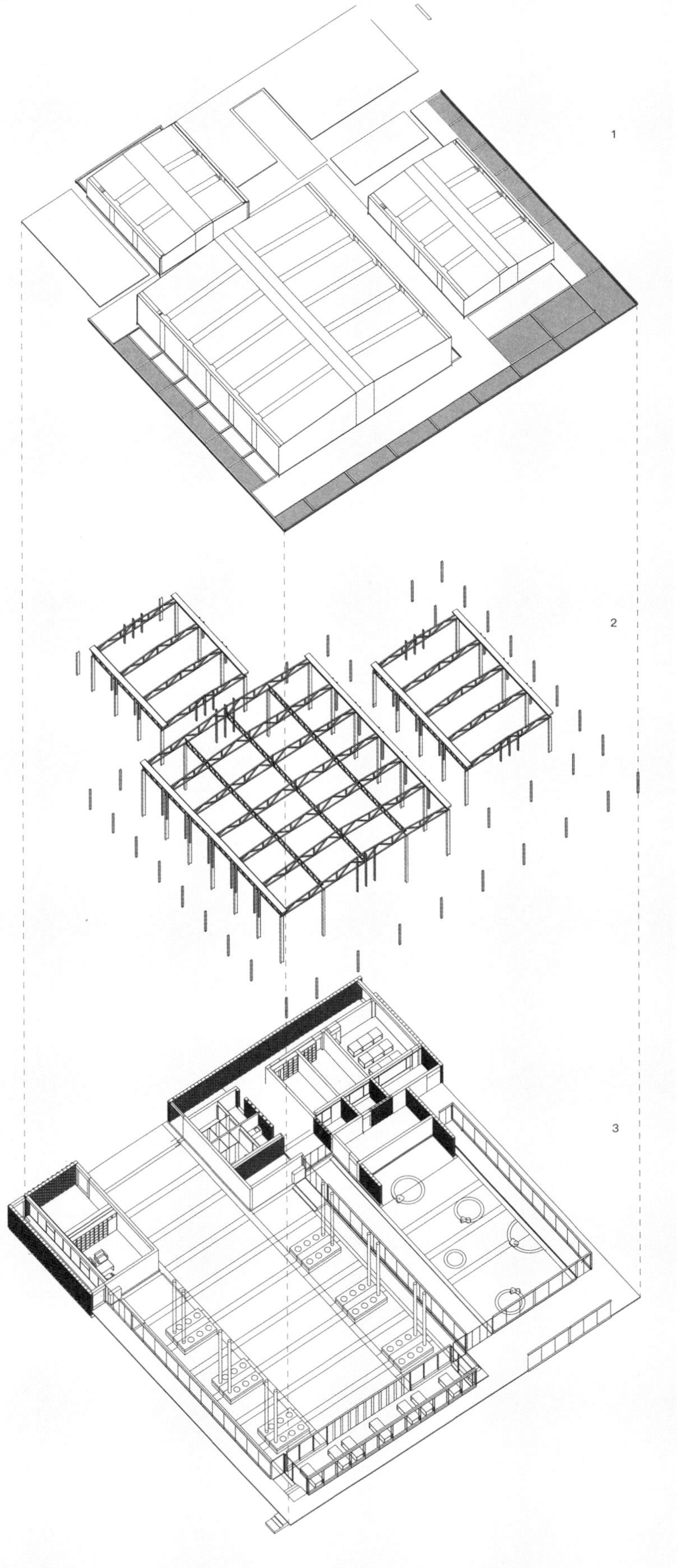

③

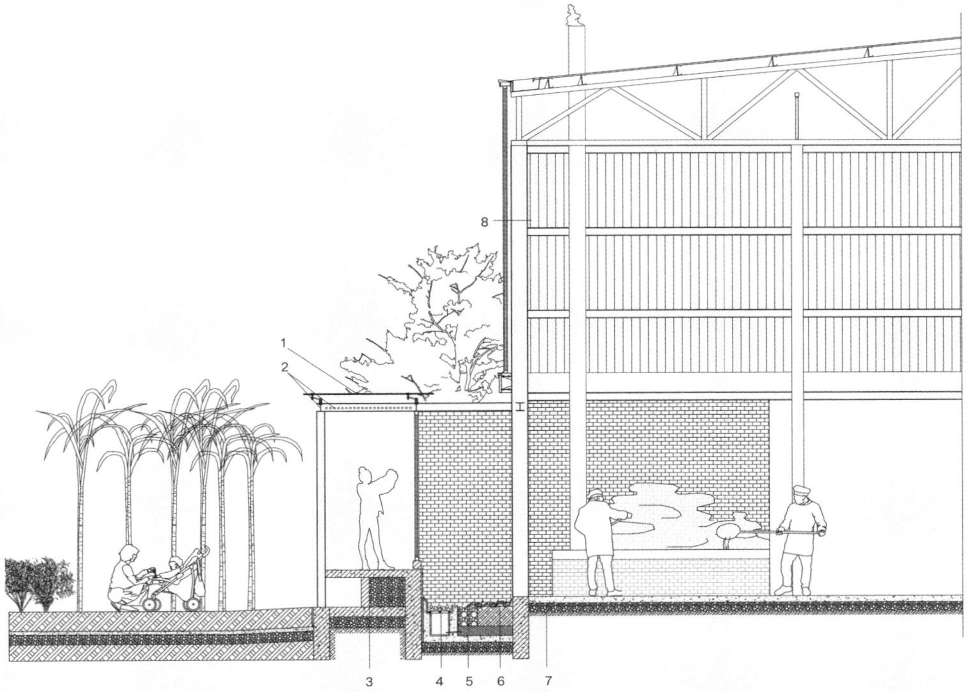

④

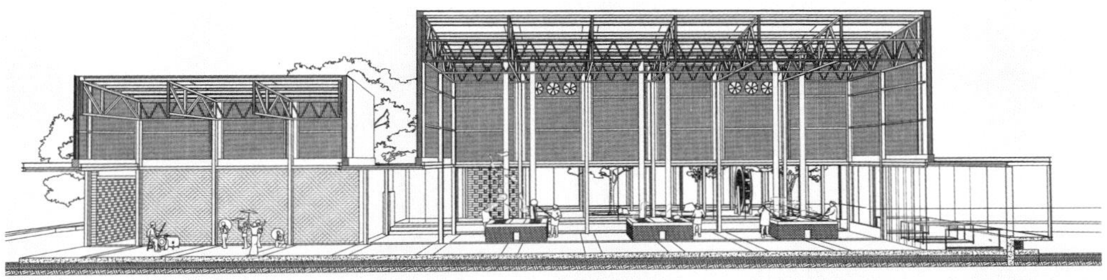

⑤

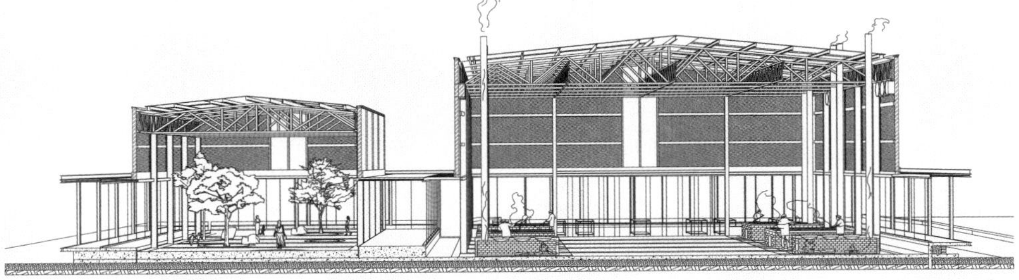

Eduard Kögel in conversation with Xu Tiantian

From Action to Concept

Eduard Kögel: You studied at Tsinghua University in Beijing and at Harvard University in the USA. Do you have your own experiences of life in rural areas? Or where does your interest in rural development come from?
Xu Tiantian: To be honest, I did not have much understanding for rural areas before Songyang. The education at Tsinghua and Harvard did not prepare me for rural areas either. In fact, our contemporary education in universities is more about urban planning and design – the rural is hardly mentioned; only when it comes to the preservation of historic buildings. When I visited Songyang for the first time, the rural appeared to me as a totally fresh and fascinating territory. In addition to the beautiful landscape, nature, tradition and culture, one must also think of the life in these villages that has been here for centuries and generations.

EK: What is the biggest challenge in rural China today?
XTT: Despite the rich culture and history, and very often the scenic beauty of these ancient villages in the landscape, local communities lack confidence in the future. When young people move to the cities for employment, the villages with very few older people become "hollow". Most rural village communities are in economic decline. There's an urgent need to revive these villages and help them regain their self-confidence.

EK: How did you prepare for working in the rural region?
XTT: When working in rural areas, it is always a learning process to discover the local culture and heritage – like an anthropologist or archaeologist – in order to connect architecture to its context.

EK: How did you come to Songyang?
XTT: Our first visit was on 8 January 2014, when we were commissioned to do a hotel project in a tea plantation. And then the county asked us to be advisors for their village projects. So we took them on as pro bono projects in the first year. For example, we proposed a bamboo pavilion to replace the original massive metal sculpture, a teahouse as a public leisure facility in the tea plantation, and a new village centre by preserving the demolished buildings in Pingtian village. This was also a learning process for us – to understand the local culture and history, which eventually led to years of more systematic collaboration.

EK: You work with various clients in Songyang. Is there such a thing as an arbitration board that mediates in conflicts, or do you have to find compromises with the local clients yourself?
XTT: Although each project has its own client, e.g. the village community sector, the municipality, or the department for tourism or culture, the overall collaboration is with the county government of Songyang. In each project, we need to communicate with both the county government and the project client in order to reach mutual agreements and understanding. Some projects require longer communication times than others.

EK: Please give us an insight into your first experience with the local craftsmen and their ideas for a new rural architecture.
XTT: Our first village project was the *Pingtian Village Centre* (p. 60). The village community wanted to demolish a cluster of abandoned buildings at the village entrance. We proposed to renew this cluster through architectural improvements to preserve the village fabric and history. Neither the villagers nor the contractor believed in the value or potential of these traditional rammed-earth-wall buildings. They were only convinced after they saw the result. By using local building materials and techniques for the renovation of these traditional houses with a new modern and public function, the improved buildings could be preserved. The local communities also had other preferences for new buildings in their villages: often copies of modern contemporary buildings from cities like Hangzhou or Shanghai. And finally this attitude has been changed by a number of new projects: the *Hakka Indenture Museum* (p. 104), the *Brown Sugar Factory* (p. 72), the *Wang Jing Memorial Hall* (p. 140), the *Tofu Factory* (p. 194), etc. Now the local villagers realise that new rural architecture doesn't have to be copied from the city. It can be something that grows from their own culture, unique, belonging only to their village. Contemporary solutions, of which the inhabitants can be proud, are necessary.

EK: What is the role of the Local Design Institute (LDI) in Songyang? Do you always work with the same institutions? Where is the interface in the planning between DnA's drafts and the LDI? Are you something like the artistic director for the LDI, or how can you ensure the quality of the execution?

XTT: Our planning system obliges us to cooperate with a Local Design Institute. Songyang Design Institute is a state-owned company that participates in CD and CA phases and provides on-site technical and structural consulting. Our engineers are not only responsible for technical support, they are also the intermediary between architects and local contractors (often from the village). Working on rural projects can lead to unexpected difficulties. A local mediator can alleviate these complications.

EK: Lighting plays an enormous role in public buildings in China. In cities, the appearance changes dramatically between day and night. You also work with a lighting design office in Songyang, and the buildings are all designed with atmospheric artificial lighting in mind. Is this a link between a contemporary city and rural areas in this respect?
XTT: The quality of light is essential to a space. It plays the main role in articulating the atmosphere and connection to its context, whether it's a space contemplating on the history or celebrating the presence. The traditional buildings and houses in Songyang have a very significant character that plays with light. When you are inside a building, you are always on the dark side and looking at the bright courtyard, mostly open to the sky. In a routine day, the lighting is always set to a dark mode that is sufficient to identify the space without interrupting the village evening. We are working with lighting designer Zhang Xin from Beijing to introduce the most efficient lighting in the villages. In certain cases, such as the *Brown Sugar Factory*, stage lighting is required during the production season, but in most other cases minimal lighting is the best solution. Not only because it's sustainable, but also to respect the quiet nights and living habits in these old villages.

EK: You have designed and built many individual projects on a village scale in the district of Songyang. This has resulted in an acupuncture strategy, setting in motion larger developments with small measures. The success of many of the small manufactories or the tourist learning networks not only improved the income of the people, they also changed the view of life in the countryside. For many years, the young people moved to the city for work, but now one can create a completely new quality of rural life with one's own or cooperative ideas. To what extent can the development in Songyang serve as a role model for others? What has to be done to ensure the success?

XTT: The architectural acupuncture strategy has become the trigger for later development in the individual village. It works with current rural tourism development and attracts visitors by restoring the identity of each village and revealing its cultural heritage. With a minimal intervention approach, multifunctional public programmes are introduced in different villages according to context and heritage. Unlike some touristic villages in the country with massive government investments, the acupuncture strategy works within a limited budget to motivate local communities to initiate further tourism or economic programmes, such as homestay businesses, local crafts workshops or organic agricultural products, all trained and facilitated via the internet. It has become a snowball effect, inspiring other villages to continue building up a regional network. This is exactly how acupuncture works: it stimulates the circulation in the system and triggers the self-healing process through minimal interventions. This self-regenerating process could be a sustainable model for other rural regions.

EK: Currently, many younger architects are working on rural projects. It seems to be a kind of experimental field for new architectural ideas. Sometimes, however, the needs of the local population seem to be overlooked and they remain excluded from the positive development, as onlookers. How can you make sure that despite the necessary investments from the city, the local population also gets a profit from the development? Are there strategies in Songyang that go beyond simple new employment opportunities to include participation in the villages?
XTT: The rural issue has become increasingly critical in recent decades, because the urbanisation process has concentrated mainly on metropolises. It's promising to see that there have recently been new societal efforts to revitalise rural areas, affecting many sectors, central and local government, corporations, investors, NGOs, artists and architects. We must also distinguish "rural projects" and "revitalising rural projects". With the increasing demand on rural tourism, more and more investment is flowing into rural areas. This could lead to another round of "rip-off" and inequality. Some of the rural projects are rather profit-oriented, such as buying up a village and resettling the villagers. Then the whole village is converted into a boutique hotel, which endangers the existence of the village and the community. In the Songyang acupuncture projects we work with tourism, but not only for

tourism. The priority is to serve the village and the community. Tourism that is integrated in local heritage and crafts, generates income and increases the viability of the village. It also works for sustainable development, where tourism is not the main purpose.

EK: Rural development has not only been neglected in China for many years. In Europe, too, countries such as Spain, Portugal or Italy are struggling with completely empty areas and a dramatic decline in the quality of life. Countries like Germany are facing shrinking rural areas in which neither work opportunities nor higher education can be found. Here, positive examples of rural development encouraging and possibly testing alternative strategies are needed urgently. Do you think that the strategies in Songyang are also interesting for other regions in China, and that these strategies can also be a positive impulse for the development of rural areas in other countries?
XTT: The Songyang strategy aims to combat local symptoms and also to develop a sustainable (and hopefully global) strategy for other rural regions. The key issue is to respect the local context and restore its rural identity. Acupuncture works multi-dimensionally: to motivate the local community, to stimulate the local economy and to attract tourism. It creates a self-healing process and eventually improves living conditions. The young generations are motivated to return from the cities to their home villages. In addition, the pleasant environment and accommodation should also attract city dwellers to visit the village life or even relocate to village living. Rural areas can offer an alternative way of life for the city dwellers if it's accessible with modern infrastructure and internet facilities.

EK: UN-Habitat in Nairobi became aware of the Songyang region through the conference "Regions on the Rise" in November 2018. What impact does this connection with a global institution have on local actors? Are there already concrete impacts and what do they look like?
XTT: Recently, UN-Habitat in Nairobi announced the Songyang Innovative Rural Development Programme as the first collaboration for sustainable rural development, and "Architectural Acupuncture" was selected as a case study for "Inspiring Practices on Urban-Rural Linkages". This introduces the Songyang experience as a global strategy that can motivate the local people and stakeholders elsewhere.

Wang Jun

Secretary of the CPC Songyang County Committee, Songyang County, China

Rural Revitalisation

From the perspective of ecological civilisation

At present, rural revitalisation is a widespread issue all over the world and the exploration of rural development is an important topic of global concern. Therefore, it is also a common concern for the fate of humanity. Today, when we discuss the topic of rural revitalisation, the first questions we must consider are: What is the fate of rural areas in the future? Is there any hope for the countryside? Which direction should be chosen for rural development in the future? Indeed, with the rapid development of urbanisation and industrialisation, a large number of villages are gradually perishing and declining. Rural decay has historical reasons and internal mechanisms. Economic and social structural adjustments led to a neglect of the countryside. Income from traditional agriculture is not sufficient for a sustainable development of villages, and skilled workers moving to the city make the situation even worse. The gap between traditional culture and a new value system adds much to this crisis.

However, with the rise of an era of ecological civilisation, we believe that rural development is full of hope. This hope comes from the modern urbanite's yearning for a rural life, from the people's desire for an intact ecological environment and healthy food, from the people's attachment to nostalgia, from the increasing adjustment of fundamental public services and the gradual improvement of modern infrastructure such as transportation and the internet. We should also recognise that, over time, the countryside will no longer be a place for agriculture only; it will also be a place of other important functions such as ecological conservation, recreation, sightseeing and a unique cultural experience, which will turn it into the new location for health care, innovation, entrepreneurship and living. Rural economic values as well as ecological, social and cultural values will become increasingly prominent.

Through our experience in the past, we understood that rural revitalisation is a large and complicated systematic project. We need to classify it against the background of the transformation from industrial civilisation to ecological civilisation. We should realise that rural development is not isolated, and that we cannot separate urban and rural areas. Also, we should start with systematic adjustments in terms of economic and social reforms.

We believe that rural revitalisation should not follow old ideas, but has to find a new way, guided by ecological civilisation, culture, quality control, a strong collective economy and common prosperity. Under the guidance of these principles, the future of the countryside should include a new kind of community, which not only maintains the original authenticity of traditional rural civilisation, but also integrates the creativity of the modern civilisation. This community's meaning and essence can be manifested in the following five new guidelines:

Firstly, a new value orientation is transforming the industrial civilisation era's people-centred, profit maximisation principles into the ecological civilisation era's credo for a harmonious relationship between humans and nature, in pursuit of a green and sustainable future. In the future, rural development will follow the concept of ecological civilisation. This includes emphasising interdependence, mutual promotion and coexistence between humans and the environment, and pursuing harmony between humanity, nature and society through sustainable production and consumption modes as well as a humane and sustainable economy.

Secondly, we need to emphasise the new urban–rural relationship. That is to say, the urban–rural duality should be transformed into an integrated city-town-village ternary symbiosis, interaction and complementation. In an era of ecological civilisation, cities and villages mutually promote each other through their coexistence. In the future, resources such as skills, capital, science and technology will be able to flow strategically between urban and rural areas, forming a new relationship with regards to economy and society.

Thirdly, we look for a new economy. The individual agricultural economy is transformed through a diverse economic pattern, based on high quality, integration and the development of agriculture, industry, trade, culture and tourism. In the future, the improvement of rural public infrastructure and the application of modern technology, such as the internet, will blur the geographical and industrial boundaries between the urban and rural areas. Traditional small agricultural businesses will evolve into comprehensive formats by promoting products, tourism, culture and creative industries. This system will grow through symbiosis and in conformity with politics, culture, society and ecology.

Fourthly, a new operating mechanism should be implemented. The old fragmented, independent and decentralised system will be transformed into a new collective economic operation mechanism that is conducive to common prosperity and corresponds with the market economy. In the future, we will establish a system based on collective economy and characterised by diverse joint cooperation and developments. Examples include joint ownership and farmer cooperatives, which can motivate individual villagers, strengthen the collective economy, guarantee a profit, achieve common prosperity and reflect collective superiority.

Fifthly, we need to refer to a new cultural system. The individual traditional farming culture will be transformed, fusing traditional local culture with modern elements and urban civilisation forms. In the future, the traditional farming culture that "respects heaven and loves people" and in which cultivation and knowledge are passed on by generations will coexist with modern philosophy, urban sciences and technology. A new culture will develop from the clash and integration of traditional and modern civilisations.

Rural decay is a dynamic process throughout history. Therefore, rural revitalisation also has to be a gradual process, which cannot be accomplished overnight. To promote rural revitalisation, we believe that the following aspects should be achieved:

Firstly, we need to establish scientific concepts. We shall fully respect the principles of rural development, instead of aiming for quick success and instant benefits. Priority should be given to existing rural resources to protect nature, ecology and the history of the countryside to the utmost and to prevent the harmonious and serene rural culture, country life and folk customs from being damaged, while gradually achieving a rural vitalisation.

Secondly, it is important to strengthen systematic construction. We should establish a holistic view, regard urban and rural development as an organic whole and promote the reciprocal flow of resources between urban and rural areas, including the construction and sharing of urban and rural infrastructure and the restoration of an ecological economy. A culture in accordance with the concept of general planning, regional linkages, systematic promotion and integrated development would support this interrelationship of urban and rural.

Thirdly, the villagers themselves should be considered as a major component. We should adhere to a development concept centred on people, welcoming visitors for holidays and accepting entrepreneurship with an open mind. But the status of the original villagers should not be changed. We should actively seek to form a union between new and existing inhabitants for the benefit of both parties. This means we must improve the organisation of the farmers and let local inhabitants have a reasonable share of the industries' benefit to ensure they profit from rural developments as much as possible.

Fourthly, we need to highlight the importance of culture. Culture is the root and soul of the countryside. It is necessary to protect, inherit and carry forward traditional culture to actively preserve and support rural culture for future generations. Creative transformation and innovative development should be combined with elements of modern civilisation and modern needs. In particular, we should fully absorb the spiritual connotation of cultures and turn it into a driver for economic and social development.

Fifthly, we need to insist on quality improvements by actively complying with the suppliers' structural requirements, craftsmanship and quality awareness throughout the rural revitalisation process, so that the countryside can become a desired place for investment. It is necessary to attract external skilled workers with ideals and local elites alike. We need to convince them to return to the countryside and participate in rural revitalisation by improving planning and design through coaching, guidance and training.

The sixth point is to strengthen social governance. Rural revitalisation is inseparable from a harmonious and stable social environment. We should improve the self-management ability and level of grass-roots organisations and actively build a rural governance system that combines autonomy, law and virtues, fosters village traditions and customs, and enhances rural cohesion.

Over the past few years, we have acted according to the philosophy "lucid waters and lush mountains are invaluable assets". We have fully implemented the development strategy of a Garden Songyang through active protection by the state and by supporting organic agriculture, revitalising the rural landscape and traditional housing, enhancing the county's economic vitality and culture, and promoting low-carbon and environmentally friendly production and lifestyles. Thus, we were able to regain rural values, improve the countryside environment and adjust the rural economy. In this process, officials and the public made joint efforts to improve our concepts and abilities. But we should be aware that there are still many upcoming challenges in the future to achieve rural revitalisation. We must thus not forget original intentions, guard ourselves against arrogance and continue to move forward!

Recently, we also made the decision to follow General Secretary Xi Jinping's 8-8 strategy for an open and prosperous countryside. We are aiming to invite the international world to our mountainous areas to develop touristic brands, such as the "Tea Town in China", "Tourism Destination for Nostalgia", "Traditional Chinese Medicine Health Resort" and the "Art and Creation Communication Resort".

We also know that this goal is extremely difficult and will take a long struggle to achieve. So we want to follow the international standards, deepen international relations, learn from international experience, set up more international development communication platforms and attract more excellent talents with an international vision and steadily promote Songyang's internationalisation development. We sincerely hope that we can receive continuous support from experts and scholars, deepen the exchange and write a new chapter for rural development.

I would also like to add that the change in Songyang is significant. The inhabitants are genuinely proud of the changes and improvements to their communities, which will hopefully lead to the further growth of the villages in the future.

Saskia Sassen

Columbia University, New York, USA

My Personal Songyang Story

How to transform a rural region into an attractive place for work and life via multiple small, but sharply delineated, insertions of stunning innovations, ranging in scale from the minute to the unexpectedly grand.

The trip from the airport to Songyang was a surprise. Down a state of the art highway with two, sometimes three lanes in each direction, and a great driver – steady, no wild driving. It was what in NYC we would think of as a high-class service: it was not about the driver, it was about the passenger's comfort – something you rarely get in a typical taxi in New York or Shanghai nowadays. And there were no crowded roads, as I have experienced so many times driving from the airport into Shanghai and Beijing. It was an *extra*-ordinary trip of almost three hours at steady speed.

We drove mostly through stunningly grand mountain scenery. It was beautiful – a feast for the eyes. The empty road made me forget about cars, it focused me on the landscape instead, the vast stretches of green and at various points beautiful mountains. We saw almost no villages or towns or cities along the way. And then we entered the town of Xiping, the administrative and cultural centre of the Songyang region. I cannot begin to describe how surprised I was; how familiar, *gemutlich*, calm, orderly and big Songyang is. A "proper city" as we might say in the West. Formally Songyang is a collection of "villages", each with its own head and history, but one experiences it as a city, not a collection of villages or as a town. That stunning emptiness along the highway had persuaded me that all that could be at the other end of the road was some rural settlement, but it turned out to be an urban space. The villages around that centre were what we were going to explore in the following days. Little did I know that what was to come would be even more surprising, stunning, engaging and unexpected.

Identity and social structure

The architect Xu Tiantian was to be my host, my guide – the source of knowledge, the bridge that would allow me to understand the innovations under way in Songyang. The next day we visited the ancient, almost abandoned centre of Wang village.

The villagers had mostly moved into three- to four-storey modern cement buildings or had left the village, leaving the old adobe houses with their wooden structures to fall apart. But since the completion of the ancestral *Wang Jing Memorial Hall* (p. 140), which Xu Tiantian had implemented, some changes had happened. A variety of new businesses had started up and the total number of inhabitants had increased from 1,500 to 2,000 since 2017. More of the old houses had been restored. One after the other, small shops and food places had opened up and tourism in Wang village went from zero to over 20,000 visitors in 2019. This is quite a success, not just economically but for the identity and social structure as well.

Not far from there we crossed *Shimen Bridge* (p. 128), which for many years had been in bad condition and closed to the public. Through the architect's intervention it now reconnected two villages, had become part of a regional tourist bike trail along the river, and instigated a new local market and little shops. With this infrastructural repair a meeting point had been created that facilitated small businesses and income. Seeing this project, I realised how it became part of a larger concept that Xu Tiantian had thrown like a net over this beautiful landscape.

A new *Teahouse* (p. 36) in the endlessly smooth and hilly tea plantations and two refurbished and modernised old adobe houses in a small village, called Pingtian, high in the mountains, became new tourist destinations with educational programmes: one offering courses relating to tea culture, production and ceremonial traditions; the other, situated in breathtaking mountainous surroundings, providing traditional dyeing courses. The neighbours had begun to refurbish their houses as well, offering places to stay overnight, and had installed coffee shops and restaurants.

Here too, within the last four years, the total number of inhabitants had increased from 20 (yes, 20!) to 160. In 2018 alone, Pingtian was visited by 12,000 tourists. This happened simply by restoring two old farmhouses in the centre of this forgotten place in the clouds and by connecting the village to a wider network of slow tourism.

Tofu and tourists

Through the winding roads down into the valley again, we went to see something that astonished me; a new type of node in Xu Tiantian's socio-economic net: the *Brown Sugar Factory* (p. 72) in Xing village and the *Tofu Factory* (p. 194) in Caizhai. Despite manufacturing different products and the fact that the tofu factory produces throughout the year while brown sugar production happens only for three months in winter, in both villages Xu Tiantian managed to unite individual families into single producers by convincing them to join together as cooperatives.

The new, contemporary buildings, which fit so well in the natural and village environment, now offered adequate hygienic production standards as well as new levels of efficiency, so that the price of the tofu increased by 50 per cent within a year. The workshops became hotspots in the new tourist concept. There were 150 per cent more visitors within one year at the tofu factory and at the sugar workshop visitor figures rose from 1,000 per year to 2,500 per month between 2016 and 2018. The price for the sugar, now available all around the region in organic food shops and online, went up by 300 per cent.

Now I understood why the editors of this book kindly persuaded me to see and to experience all this. It is impossible to read from numbers, images or videos what has been knitted together here by an architect and a progressive local government.

Effectiveness and beauty

On the last day, before rushing back to Shanghai and then via Europe to New York, we saw DnA's *Hakka Indenture Museum* (p. 104). Once again cultural heritage was the point of departure for this wonderful place made of natural stone embedded in a beautiful valley. The realisation of this museum instigated a number of conversions of old farmhouses in the vicinity into homestay and other tourism facilities, which brought a growth in visitors from around 700 to 5,000 per month as it stands today. The population decline was also halted and then followed by a slow rise. In the course of this amazing trip, I saw numerous small and large developments. It was something I have never seen with this level of effectiveness or beauty before. The number of projects Xu Tiantian has developed is extraordinary. But what is even more unexpected is the range of her interventions – literally from the grand to the miniscule. In all my travels to both remote and familiar destinations, I have never faced such a variety and quantity of such interventions by an architect in a period of only five years. It is a magnificent way to bring life to a remote town, a small city, a major city, a village or a building.

All these have made more and more people stay in the region instead of migrating to the big cities. There is even a small number of people (around 6,000 over the last five years) who have moved back there from the big cities, which is a big success for the rural society of the region, as well as for its economic independency. Of course, it has to be taken into account that a lot of money was and will be spent on the infrastructure: highways, a regional airport, high-speed internet – all well invested from my point of view.

A range of interventions

Stepping back and trying to decode the sense of it all, it became clear to me that some of the smaller interventions might be overlooked by the casual passer-by. One is stunned by the beauty and care (and effectiveness) of these often really tiny transformations. Often, something will catch your eye as you walk past that makes you go back to check it out. And there is this carefully, beautifully shaped insert of a bit of wood and glass, in many diverse variations.

As the days went by and I saw more and more of them, it struck me how one outcome of this range of interventions was the opening up of what is typically not opened up in an urban setting.

Glass and light-coloured wood emerged as crucial actors in these transformations. The effectiveness of this recurrent mix and coloratura is what impressed me – both in its capacity to bind settings big and small and in its lightness of touch. It reminds me of the effectiveness of the old small cities in European history, which coded themselves in diverse ways: the gates of the town, the height and colours of the buildings, and more. Such interventions can be constitutive, enabling a sense of connectivity and membership.

What I saw in Songyang was a model of intervention we rarely see in our cities today. It bordered on the unbelievable given its range of scale – from tiny to grand – with the same span of effects on the social and economic life on its inhabitants.

Xu Tiantian and Saskia Sassen at Wang Jing Memorial Hall

Hakka Indenture Museum

Shicang Village 2017

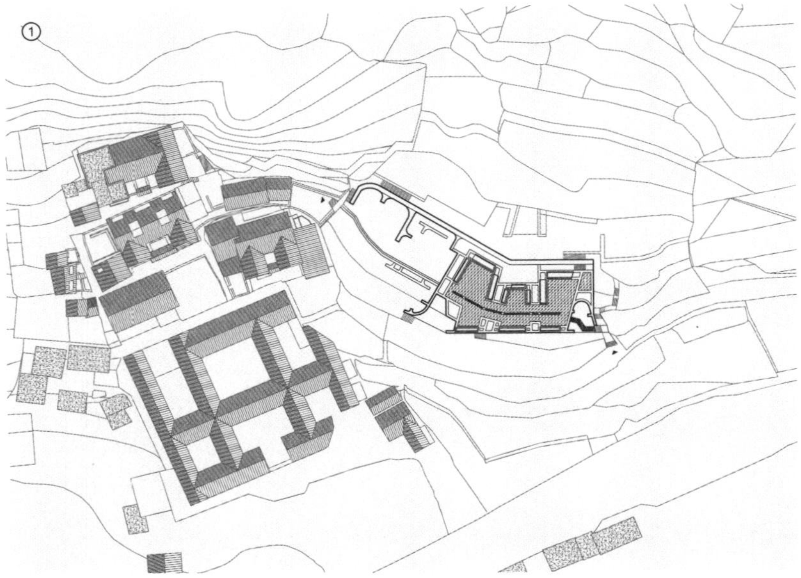

The Hakka Indenture Museum is located in a narrow valley in the south of Songyang County. It was built by Xu Tiantian at the edge of Shicang village, whose residents belong to a Hakka ethnic group. The Hakka migrated here as refugees from northern regions in the past centuries. They have retained their special status to this day, which is characterised by the strong internal cohesion of the group.

The name of the village, Shicang, can be translated as "stone storage". It refers to a legend about a magical cave filled with grain, which supplied the residents. Greedy inhabitants allegedly broke open the cave, which consequently lost its ability to produce grain. Afterwards only stones were to be found there.

To commemorate Hakka history, Xu Tiantian developed a building that employs the local method used for constructing bridges and residential buildings. Coarsely hewn stones are layered in a wild pattern to create massive walls that continue the slope at the edge of the village out into the neighbouring environment. The architecture is connected with the landscape by means of various sequences of spaces both inside and out. A pre-existing irrigation channel was guided over the roof to provide water that is sprayed through nozzles to form a water curtain on the inside. By means of a linear opening in the roof, sunlight falls on the water curtain, creating a rainbow. This temporary phenomenon attracts visitors, thereby also enlivening the neighbouring villages. The museum itself has no controlled access and exhibits copies of, in part, Hakka indentures that are several hundred years old, as well as specially produced woodcarvings depicting Hakka history. The inspiration from the local legend determines the museum, revitalising both craftsmanship and material culture.

Client: People's Government of Xing Village in Songyang County

① Site plan
② Axonometric drawing
③ Front elevation
④+⑤ Section

②

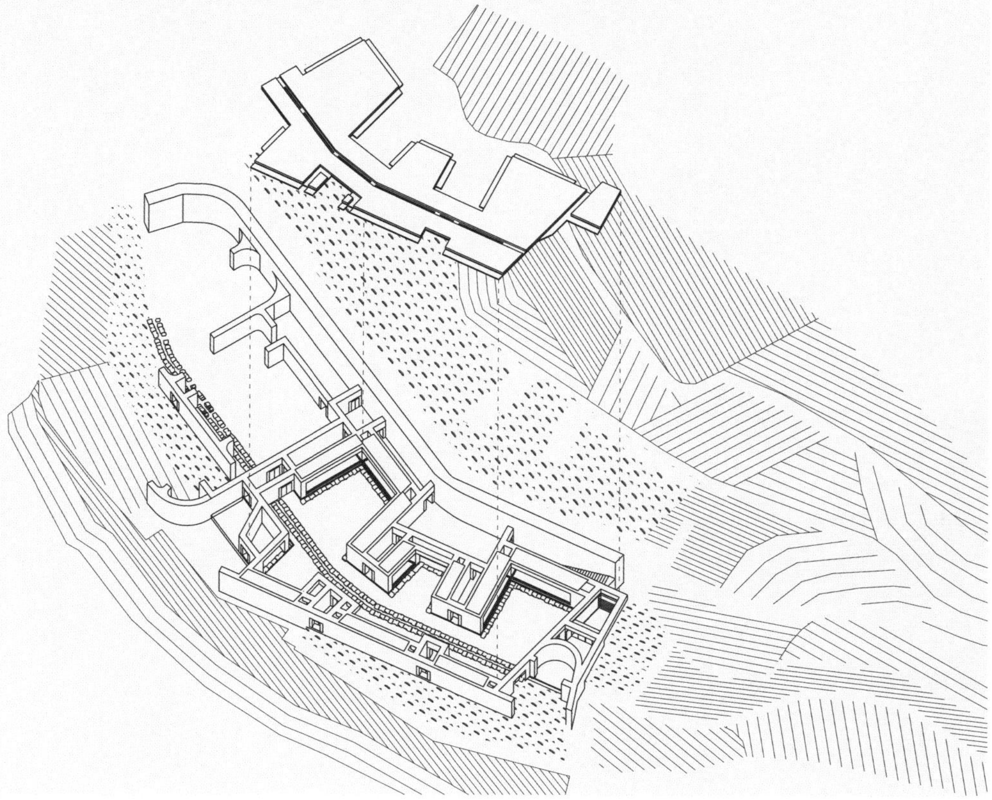

③

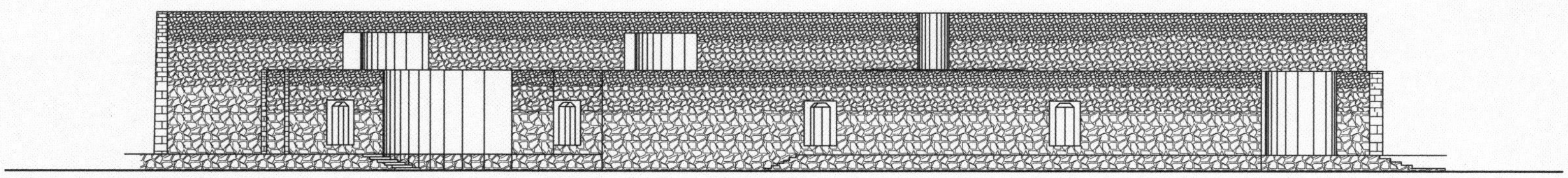

④

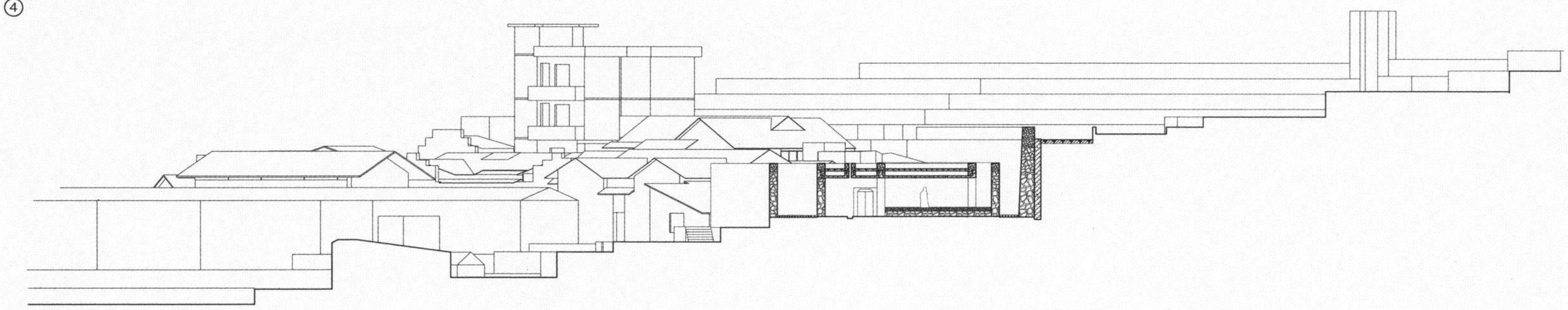

⑤

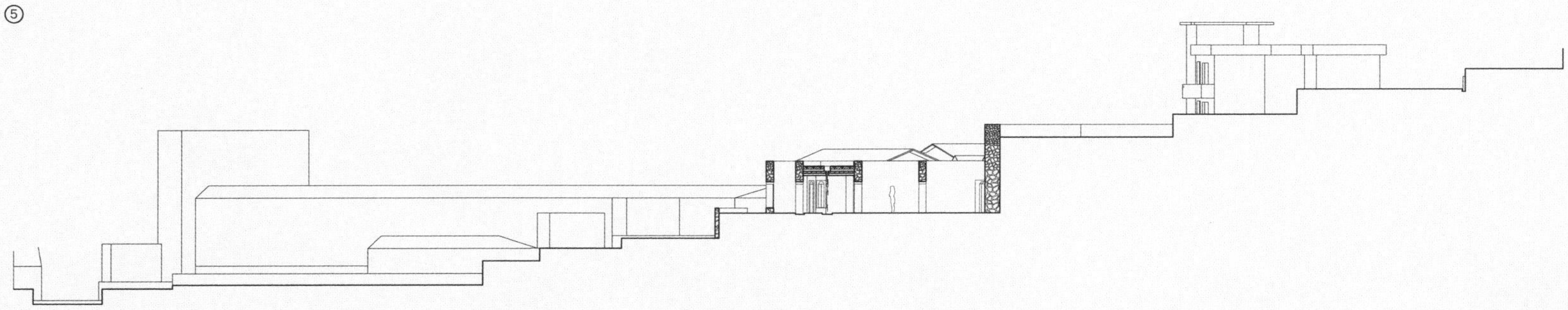

Pine Park Pavilion

Huangyu Village 2017

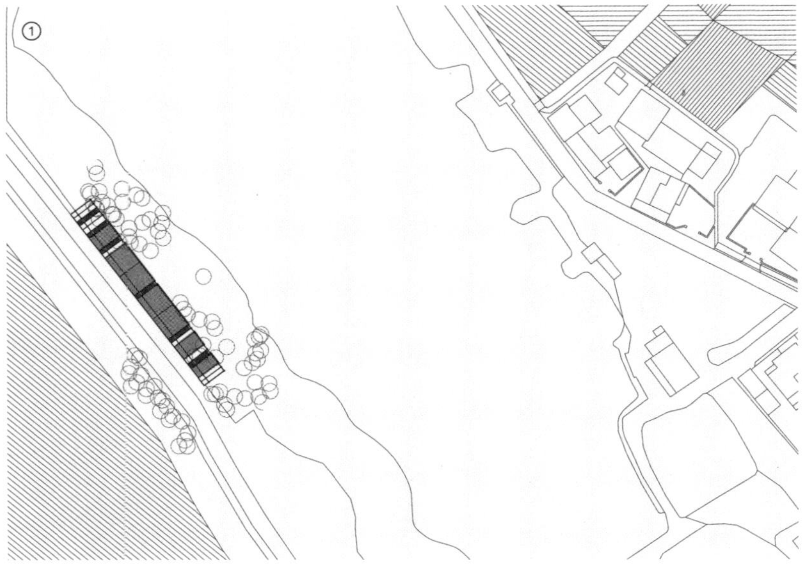

This pavilion is located next to the village of Huangyu on a paved path along the Songyin River and serves as an attraction for locals and tourists alike, inviting cyclists and hikers to rest and learn about specific aspects of the region's economy. The wooden structure consists of prefabricated elements, which were assembled on site, and accommodates an art installation representing the historical production of pine resin.

The elongated pavilion consists of five segments, each with different functions: a pavilion for storage, a retail store, toilet facilities, a private space for the management and a public tea room. The building elements are separated by glass panes, on which the resin production is artistically represented and thus merges with the existing pine trees around the pavilion to form a poetic image that borrows from nature. Four of the pavilions are completely transparent; only the toilet facilities are covered with wooden panels.

All components – the structure, the ceilings and floors, and the built-in furniture – are made of wood, adding to the perception of the pavilion cluster as a frame for the view across the beautiful river landscape.

Client: Songyang Department of River Control and Reservoir Management

① Site plan
② Axonometric drawing
1 private room; 2 tea room;
3 rest room; 4 retail store;
5 pavilion
③ Ground floor
④ Section

②

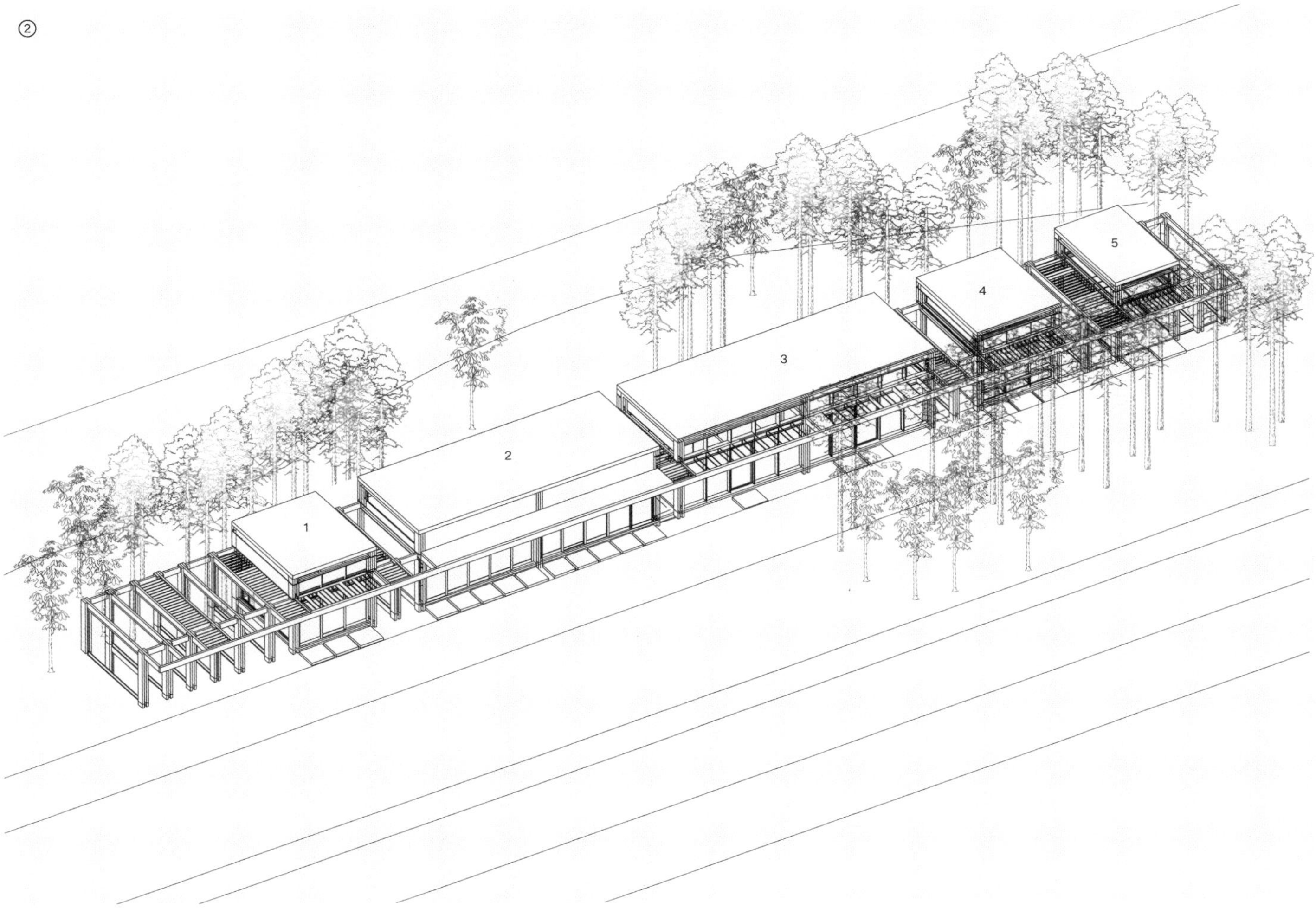

③

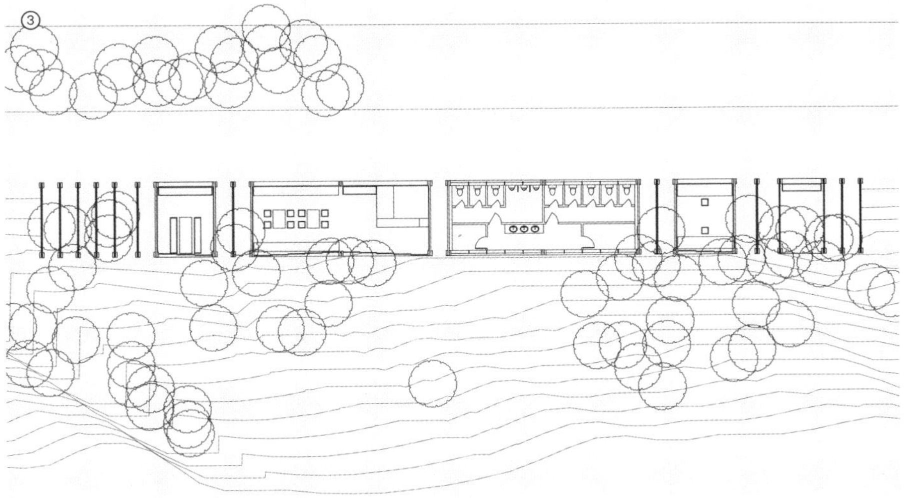

④

Shimen Bridge

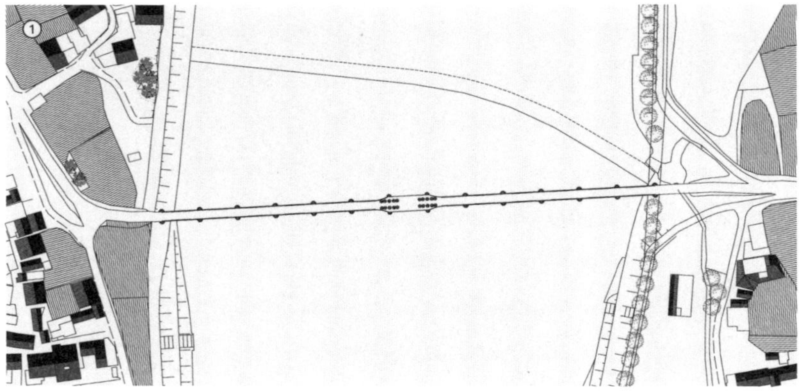

Shimen Village 2017

This bridge over the Songyin River links the villages of Shimen and Shimenyu. The existing stone masonry bridge with its characteristic 13 arches dates from the 1950s and was closed for vehicles for many years due to structural defects. With the renovation and modernisation of the bridge, Xu Tiantian has designed a social place that reconnects the two villages not only physically but also from a cultural point of view. The result is a roofed bridge space reminiscent of Wind and Rain Bridges, a type of bridge building with a long tradition in China. These historical roofed bridges had a social and cultural significance that was taken up by the architect.

A culturally and historically important dam system that has regulated the water of the Songyin River for 1,500 years, as part of a larger system across the whole valley, can be seen from the bridge. As part of the new cycle path along the river, the bridge connects the two banks and allows a round trip.

For the new roof, Xu Tiantian designed a simple wooden prefabricated element, defining the space on the bridge in additive sequences. In the middle, a square planted with trees invites the traveller to spend time. The visual connection to the river and – even more – the cultural elevation of the bridge, helps the two neighbouring villages to define a shared cultural space, making it possible to experience their historical link in a new way. The residents took possession of the bridge immediately and regularly hold markets there that attract many visitors. With few means, a new public space was created from infrastructure that had become unusable, bringing together both the local population and visitors.

Client: Songyang Public Road Administration

① Site plan
② Axonometric details
③ Axonometric drawing

②

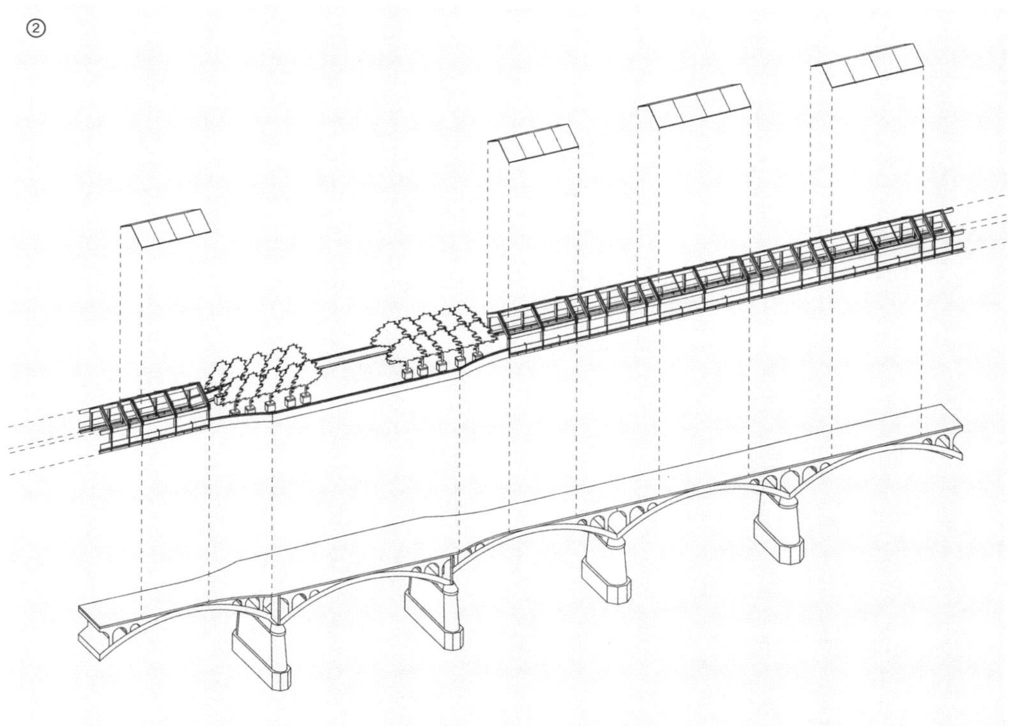

③

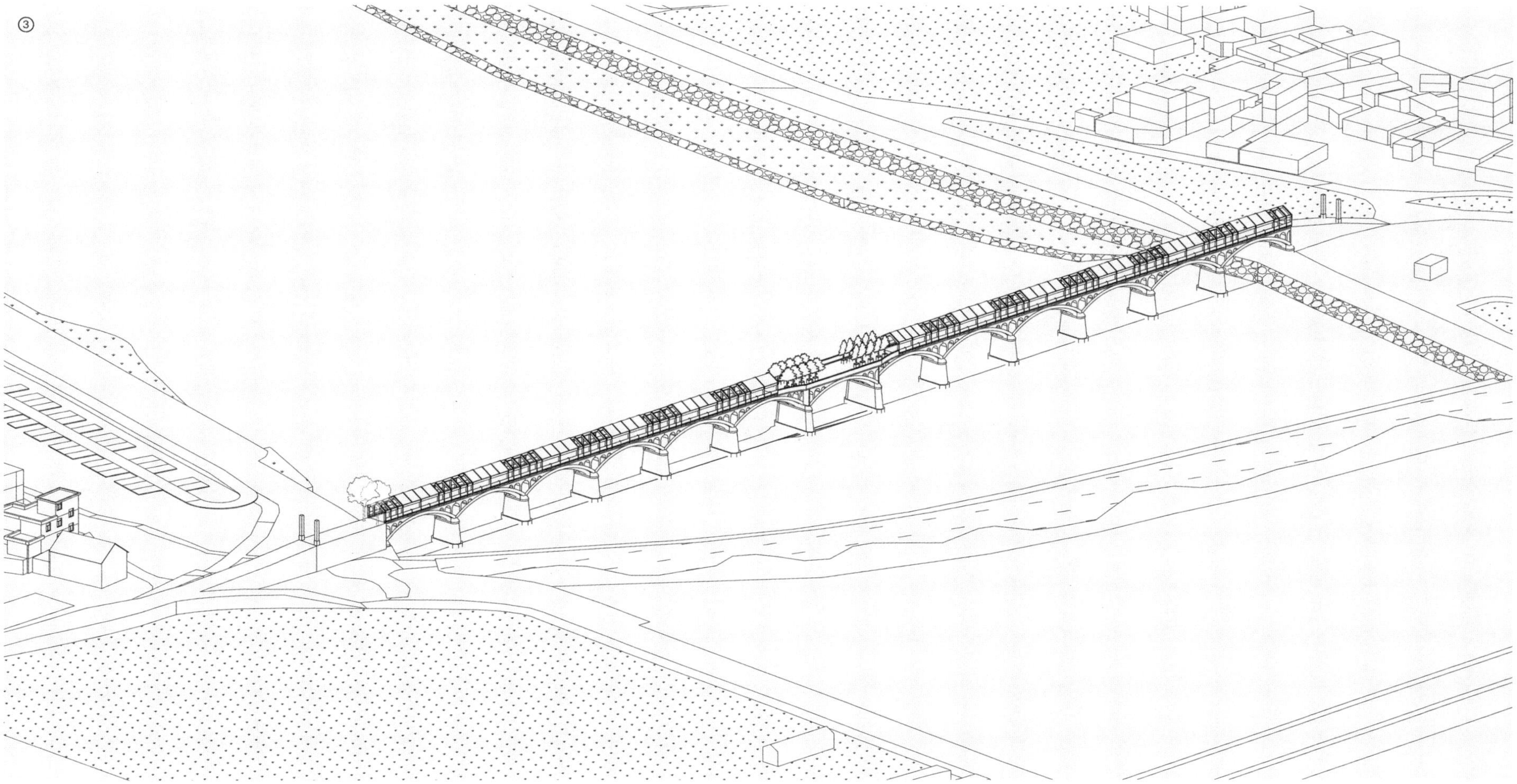

A0390
A0401

Wang Jing Memorial Hall

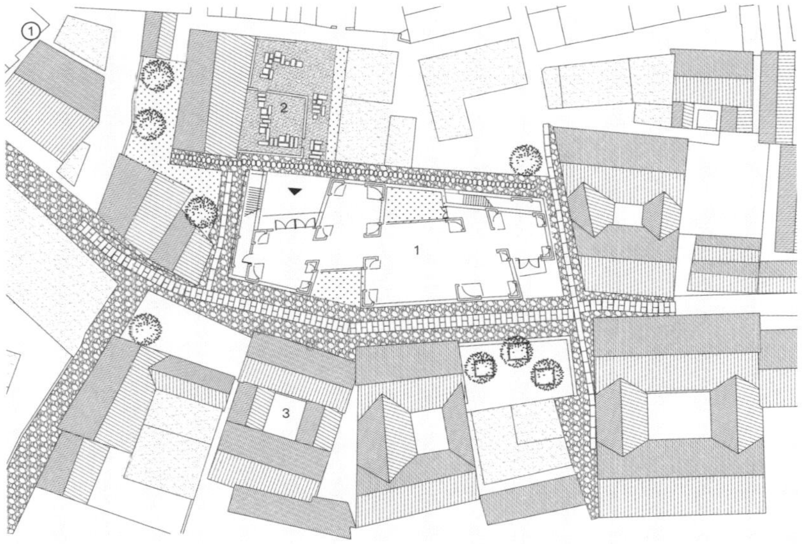

Wang Village 2017

The village council of Wang, where the influential scholar Wang Jing was born in 1337, decided to build a memorial hall opposite the ancestral temple to commemorate the life of its famous former resident. Wang Jing rose to become the advisor of the first emperor of the Ming Dynasty, was a member of the Hanlin Academy and was involved in compiling the *Yongle Encyclopedia* in 1408, the most comprehensive summary of knowledge in China at the time.

The region's historical trade route runs between the ancestral temple and the new building. Before construction, most of the old buildings in the village, made of rammed earth with an internal wood structure supporting the roof, were in poor condition, and even the ancestral temple was on the verge of collapse.

For the new building, Xu Tiantian developed a linear building structure that fits organically into the layout of the old village and mediates between the old, one-storey rammed earth structures and the two- to three-storey concrete and tiled farmers' buildings of recent years. Since building regulations prescribe reinforced concrete for the load-bearing structure of the building, only the outer walls are made of rammed earth. The constructive framework of the new memorial hall comprises open concrete elements defining the 17 corners of the layout and letting light and air into the building from above. Here the life of Wang Jing is depicted in hand-carved raised stone reliefs. Thanks to this building, which is also used as a centre for the village community, old construction techniques and local crafts have been revived.

Client: Songyang Wansong District, Wang Village Council

① Site plan
1 Wang Jing Memorial Hall; 2 public courtyard;
3 ancestral temple

② Axonometric drawing
1 entrance; 2 villager meeting room; 3 patio;
4 commemorative columns; 5 public courtyard

③ Sectional perspective

④+⑤ Section

⑥ Depiction of the life of Wang Jing in 17 reliefs

②

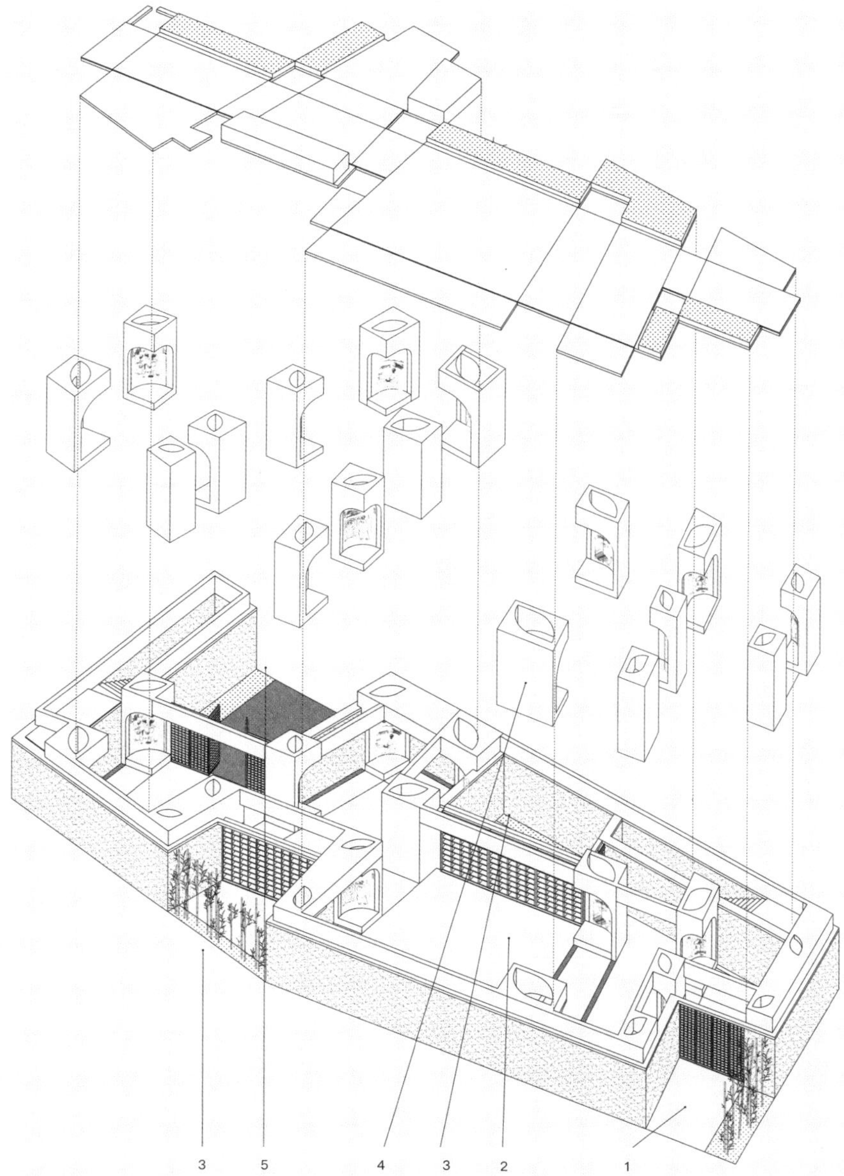

③

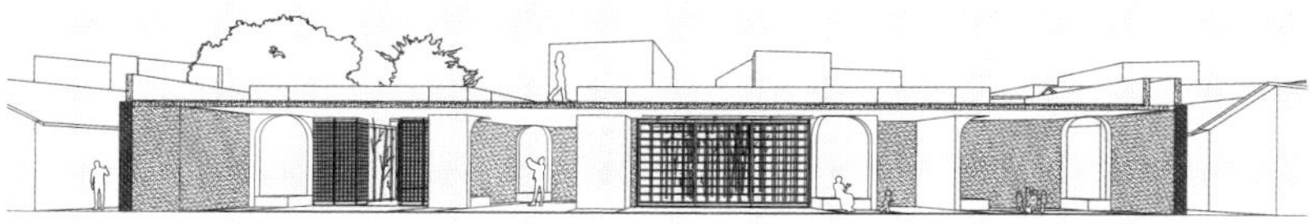

④

⑤

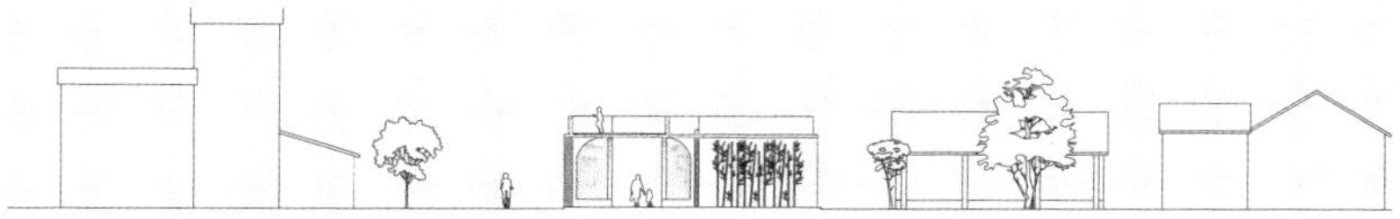

⑥

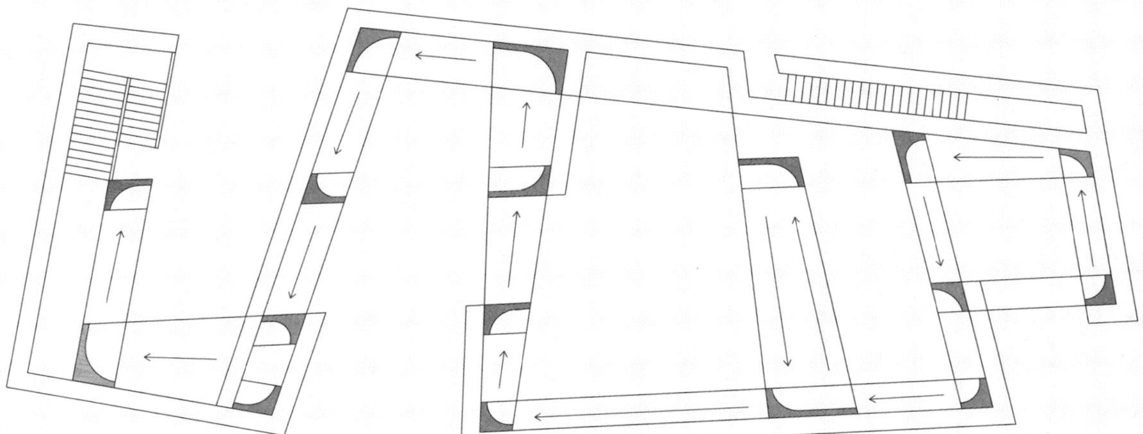

葉氏宗祠

参政山西

Camellia Oil Workshop

Hengzhang Village, Songyang 2018

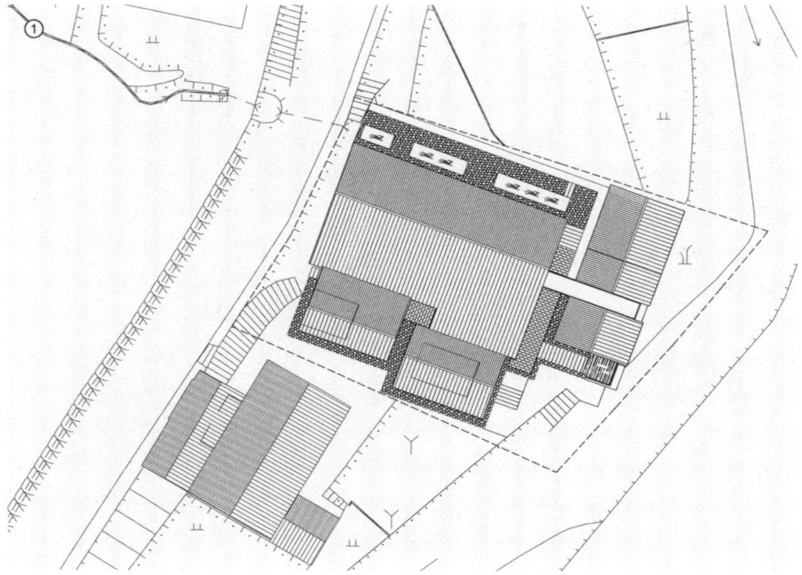

The Camellia Oil Workshop building complex is located in Hengkeng village, administered by Dadongba Town and embedded in a mountainous landscape covered with bamboo forests. As is ubiquitous in this region, the buildings consist of a post-and-beam construction with wooden joints supporting the roof. The walls of the buildings are mainly made of rammed earth and the terrace walls are made of natural stone taken from the riverbed.

In former times, the camellia oil from Hengkeng village was very well known in the area. The old workshop complex, abandoned for decades, was built over a hundred years ago in the valley next to a fast-flowing small stream.

In autumn 2017, it was decided to revive the old camellia oil plant as a production and leisure site for locals and tourists. First, the existing buildings and wooden machines were secured and repaired. Then a new kitchen, a packing room and a leisure pavilion by the stream were built. The new components were constructed using the old technique, and the walls were set with cut oval fieldstones integrating the building complex into the landscape of the retaining walls. The annexes were composed of overlapping pitched roofs, which form a roof landscape and provide ventilation and lighting for the interiors.

The new building was constructed with local materials and know-how; it fits perfectly into both the context and the limited budget. The cut stones of the surrounding wall set a contemporary sign in the traditional building composition. In addition, this small intervention also created a new source of income for the villagers.

Client: People's Government of Dadongba Town

① Site plan
② Axonometric drawing
1 kitchen; 2 production room; 3&7 visitors' passage; 4 outdoor platform; 5 exhibition/production area; 6 oil pressing area; 8 scenic spot
③ Side elevation
④ Sectional perspective
⑤ Ground floor plan
1 exhibition; 2 kitchen; 3 tea cake manufacture; 4 oil manufacture; 5 tasting area

②

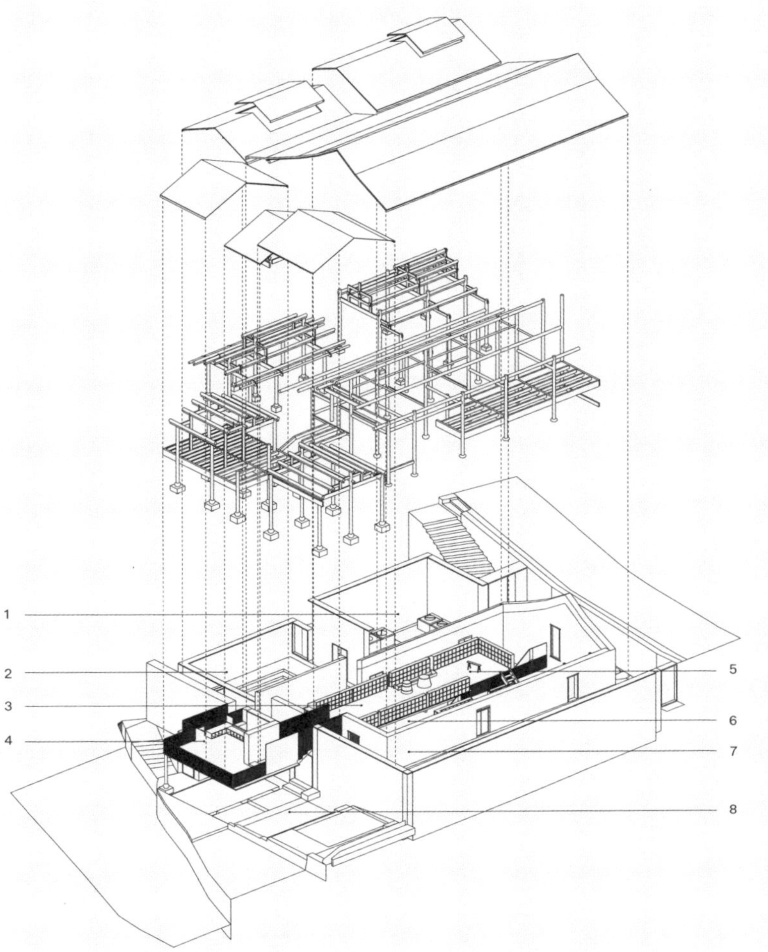

③

④

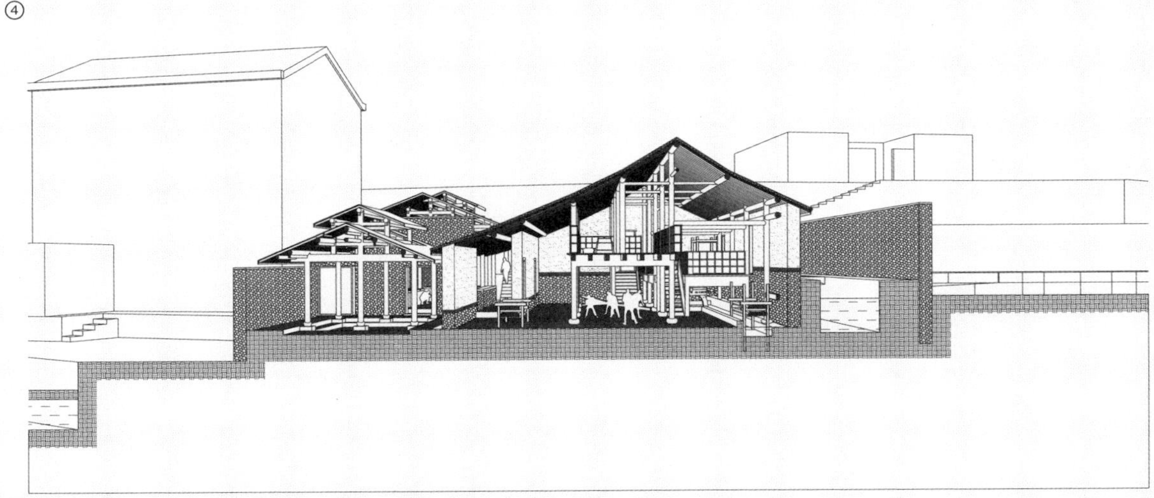

⑤

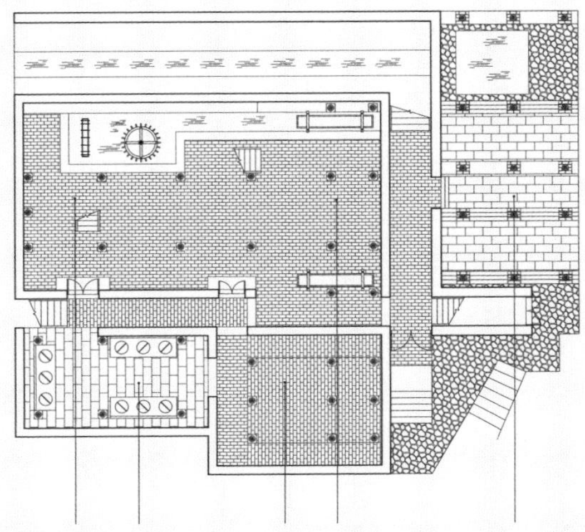

Eduard Kögel

Potentials and Challenges

Today, about 20 per cent of the world's population lives in China, but the country accounts for less than 10 per cent of the world's agricultural land, meaning that huge increases in productivity are needed to feed the population.

This is being achieved through the industrialisation of agriculture. But the pressure on the ecosystem is immense, which puts the security of food production at risk. New ecological approaches and an improved communication between producers and consumers are needed. Other challenges include water and air pollution, deforestation and human habitat loss. For the development of rural communities, it is necessary to support new initiatives and stimulate the creative industries to find new solutions with old know-how. Sustainable tourism requires the preservation of historical structures as well as technical infrastructure for mobility and hygiene. It is also necessary to analyse where the contradictions between the expectations of the urban population and local potential lie. A productive approach to functional problems is needed here. But the local population must also be culturally and aesthetically involved, so that the new buildings do not remain mere decoration. In Songyang County, the local administration, political leadership, residents and planners have set themselves the task of tackling some of these challenges using architectural means – therefore architects must be innovative in order to take the villagers on a new adventure.

Natural and cultural potentials

Songyang is a county dominated by mountains and the Songyin River valley. It contains more than 400 villages and circa 240,000 inhabitants. It is located in the southwest of Zhejiang Province and the provincial capital of Hangzhou is 270 kilometres away. New transport infrastructures with motorways and high-speed trains have catapulted this agrarian county into a new era, since the large cities of Shanghai and Hangzhou can now be reached relatively quickly. An airport is also under construction in the nearby city of Lishui, which is due to open in

2021 and expected to handle one million passengers per year by 2025. As part of the technical infrastructure, access to the internet, through which a lot of day-to-day business takes place, has become well established in Songyang – even in its more remote mountain villages.

The large valley of the Songyin River, and the steeply ascending mountains that surround it, shape the landscape. For the more than 70 – still largely traditional – villages it encompasses, Songyang County has set up a programme to revitalise rural communities. The different types – villages along the river, terraced villages on the slopes, villages of the Hakka ethnic group in the mountains, or in the gorge – present a broad spectrum of local settlement typology, each with its own characteristics. Today, over 1,000 buildings in this county are protected. There are over 200 ancestral temples, 20 historical covered Wind and Rain Bridges, and 60 kilometres of historical paths, which have already been repaired. The temples of Confucius, Guan Yu (known in the West as a god of war), or the heavenly goddess Mazu (Tianhou) are also receiving renewed attention. Structures that are important supra-regionally, such as the wooden, tilted Yanqing pagoda from the ninth century (Song dynasty), not only bear witness to the long historical significance of the region but also are listed as national cultural assets and as important monuments in the history of architecture.

In the villages, it is still possible to find local craftspeople with specific knowledge and skill sets that will disappear if their trades do not succeed in adapting to current needs. The diversity of village cultures and the differentiated local particularities give Songyang County a good basis, which local politicians would like to do justice to with a bespoke strategic concept.

Today, the history of the region and its outstanding figures are also being reassessed and repositioned with regard to local self-perception. The poet Zhang Yuniang (1250–1277), the Taoist wonder worker Ye Fashan (631–720) and the scholar Wang Jing (1337–1408) all contribute to a deep historical rootedness in talented ancestors. New buildings and a new appreciation now ascribe them their place in local significance. For example, Xu

Tiantian has adapted a new building dedicated to the memory of Wang Jing into the context of the village structure (*Wang Jing Memorial Hall* (p. 140)), along with a museum for poetry, in which the thirteenth-century poet Zhang Yuniang will be remembered.

Over past centuries, Songyang has also served as a place of retreat for innumerable Hakka families, who had lost their official status with the administration and suffered persecution by the rulers. The mountainous region offered hiding places for the Hakka, but these refugees also needed to come to terms with the local population. This story can be told with the contracts that the local inhabitants concluded with the immigrants. Xu Tiantian has built a museum for these contracts as well, which invites discourse on the subject. This is relevant because the issue is still important today – integration and demarcation between those who are already here and newcomers still has to be negotiated.

Garden, farm and recreation

The demand from cities for safe food and the search for recreational landscapes for the middle classes are opening up new perspectives for development that can only be implemented on the basis of complex concepts and the small-scale structures in the villages. Local politicians are therefore searching for economically sustainable solutions that do not just materialise in the short term, but also contribute to long-term development at a regional level as a result of the interplay of various measures. Moreover, it is hoped that people returning from the cities will recognise the improving situation and play a part in the renewal of rural regions with their inventive skills and investments.

Excellent agricultural products are cultivated in Songyang, and with the politically supported transition to organic farming in the future, farmers will be able to satisfy the new needs of the urban middle classes. In order to be effective in the long term, however, a large-scale education strategy is needed to provide the local population with new knowledge about organic farming. This too will require future investments. The outstanding position of the local tea production facilitates a qualitative diversification that reassesses traditional knowledge, making it accessible for new products. Naturally, price development also plays a decisive role in work-intensive ecological production. However, early examples confirm the hope that new economic framework conditions can revitalise rural life here in the future.

Besides agriculture, the region also has great potential as a recreational landscape. The Songyin River Greenway is being developed strategically as a regional cycle path along the river with a range of leisure activities. Here, the architect Xu Tiantian has constructed, for instance, a small pavilion providing information about historical resin production. At other places along the cycle path she has designed a water centre, the *Qinglongyan Visitors' Lounge* and the *Dalutan Blueberry Pavilion*, providing further attractions and information about the local area. The path branches off into tea plantations where pavilions and teahouses offer cyclists variety and recreation in a landscape characterised by small-scale agriculture, whose backdrop is dominated by the surrounding mountains.

Simple, high-quality homestays with a cosy atmosphere in redeveloped historical village buildings present a rustic alternative to the polished appearance of large urban hotels. Local offers have been created in cooperation with local restaurants, providing farmers with an additional income. The picturesque views from many villages in the mountains have inspired amateur painters and photographers, since the topographical situation and its natural meteorological phenomena, such as fog, low-lying clouds and clear blue skies, provide a special environment for such activities.

Next steps

The prerequisites necessary for developing a rural creative industry are under discussion. The main question is how to lure talents from the big cities to rural regions. To this end, there will surely need to be further experiments in the future looking into how a rural creative industry, beyond arts and crafts, can be promoted. What is necessary for this is in-depth knowledge of local structures, techniques and history – in short, an archiving of local wisdom – as a basis upon which something new can emerge. In addition, an ecological approach that supports the rural atmosphere and keeps the historical coexistence between nature and culture apparent has become visible in current demonstration projects. Furthermore, new fields of work have to be created, and education and training need to be oriented towards global discourses. A school for rural know-how concerned with practical local examples might give rise to new approaches to develop customised solutions in cooperation with the population.

The work of Xu Tiantian, but above all the work of the local population, administration and politicians, helps to create a new perspective for rural development, which in the case of Songyang has already inspired returnees from the big cities to see future potential again in their home villages. As a precedent, this method tested in Songyang of building new self-confidence with architecture will also be of great importance elsewhere.

Remy Sietchiping

Chief of Policy, Legislation, and Governance Section, Urban Practices Branch,
Global Solutions Division, UN-Habitat

Grounding the 2030 Agenda

Guiding principles of urban–rural linkages

Abstract

Humanity has a duty to reduce poverty and inequality to improve living conditions for all. The "leaving no one and no place behind" policy proposes an agenda and initiatives to accomplish these bold, but essential actions. Embracing this initiative will ensure that social and spatial equities are safeguarded for all, prosperity is shared, the protection of the environment is better regulated and nurtured, and greater efforts in adaptation and mitigation are proposed to reduce constructed and natural risks and disasters.

There are many proven approaches and tools available to foster inclusive development and synergies for all people and places. Sustainable Development Goals (SDGs), integrated territorial development, inclusive growth, architectural acupuncture, the urban–rural linkages guiding principles and its framework for action, are all relevant frameworks. When the linkages to create more synergies are weak, there should be a greater incentive to create opportunities and leverage the catalytic role of marginalised groups and neglected urban, peri-urban and rural areas.

My ultimate desire is to have a functional ecosystem that promotes the health and well-being of households in interdependent urban, peri-urban and rural areas. In this paper, I outline some of the challenges of translating policy into real change on the ground. I draw from the Songyang experience with regard to the project's ingredients for success and consider its replicability. I conclude by underscoring the role of various stakeholders and partners in identifying and promoting inspiring practices.

From policy intentions to real change

The policy/action interface offers a glimpse of the necessity for positive change in people's lives. Global and national policies, regulations, frameworks and strategies are well-drafted and presented. The *2030 Development Agenda* is an example of a global covenant of nations working together at a very local level to advocate changes and actions for a better humanity. It is not a particularly easy task to assess the effectiveness of SDGs and other well-intended policy goals that have actual, on the ground, applicable actions that can make a tangible difference in individuals' lives. For instance, those living in deprived rural areas or neighbourhoods in urban and peri-urban areas are less resilient to economic, social and environmental shocks. Policy intentions often ensure that development positively impacts the whole territory or country and reaches the maximum number of citizens. Approaches such as "architectural acupuncture" have been used to identify, promote and scale successful projects through tailored local interventions that have a ripple effect over a large territory, and consequently impact a larger pool of people.

The Songyang experience: why and how are these projects transformative?

In November 2018, I was invited to present at "Regions on the Rise: Culture and Architecture as Drivers for Rural Development" in China, an international conference hosted by Songyang County and Aedes Architecture Forum & Network Campus Berlin. Songyang County is a rural area under the administration of Lishui City in Zhejiang Province, located southwest of Shanghai. The conference was an opportunity to showcase successful architectural interventions in rural areas that have had catalytic effects beyond the project sites.

Whilst in Songyang, I observed that the transformative experience there clearly demonstrates the role of rural development within the continuum of human settlements to ensure that "no one and no place is left behind". This was a practical example of implementing the SDGs. Additionally, my visit coincided with UN-Habitat leading a partnership to advance global effort towards making urban–rural linkages a reality. Since we were looking for ways to "localise" the SDGs and actualise the

Urban-Rural Linkages Guiding Principles (URL-GP), I felt encouraged that the Songyang experience was a working example for grounding these global frameworks. It also illustrated that carefully designed interventions in rural areas can trigger a domino effect of development that can impact peri-urban and rural areas. I observed that selected architecture revitalisation interventions in the urban areas could benefit the rural population. Projects such as the *Tofu Factory* (p. 194) and the *Brown Sugar Factory* (p. 72) had positive trickle-down effects on the area's food and nutrition systems that extended beyond the county's borders.

Based on the territorial food system approaches, it is clear that in Songyang County food security and a healthy diet are closely related to land, water, waste, health, culture and heritage. Through the network created between these different elements, the revitalisation projects were designed to support smallholder farmers, craftspeople, actors in the local food chain and consumers in territorial markets.

In implementing various acupuncture projects in Songyang, the role of national as well as local leadership is evident. The central government of China, in addition to local county governments, has explicit policies and programmes that are directed towards revitalising deprived areas. The local political leadership plays a key role in identifying innovative ways to transform these deprived areas into attractive and vibrant spaces. Another important component in implementing these interventions is the passion and genuine care of Xu Tiantian, a Beijing-based architect and the chief designer of major transformative projects in Songyang County. Xu Tiantian and her company, DnA_Design and Architecture, have been instrumental in applying the architectural acupuncture approach towards transforming Songyang County's territories and the lives of its residents. The architecture acupuncture chefs-d'œuvre she has created here are directly associated with the well-being and reputation of those residing in Songyang County. Through the commitment of local county leadership, local expertise, and coordination and collaboration with the residents, responsibilities were shared for these interventions and projects in order to transform them from visions into reality. From this learning experience in Songyang

County, I can conclude that visionary, transformative and distributive leadership is essential for policy intentions to lead to actionable change.

Why collaborate on practices?

Since local context and realities often influence measures of success, there are different lessons that can be drawn from, adapted to or applied to other transformative projects in the pipeline. UN-Habitat aims to go beyond documenting and disseminating “good” urban practices by showcasing how such innovative interventions can contribute to the revitalisation of rural areas and protect the environment through empowering the local people technically, financially and mentally. In collaboration with Songyang County, UN-Habitat seeks to leverage successful cases such as Songyang’s rural development projects to provide valuable lessons and inspiration for other rural areas worldwide. Equally, best practices from other rural districts in China and beyond can also stimulate further innovations in Songyang County and around the globe. Innovative and sustainable development initiatives are expected to substantially strengthen rural areas and their linkages to cities, relieve the demographic pressure of urban areas and contribute extensively to the overall prosperity of human settlements.

UN-Habitat’s *Strategic Plan 2020–2023* aims to “improve living conditions for all” by “reduc[ing] inequality and poverty in communities across the urban-rural continuum”, and “enhance[ing] shared prosperity of cities and regions”. Furthermore, issues regarding social inclusion with respect to gender, children, youth, older people and the disabled, which predominantly occur in rural areas, will be taken into full consideration. It was agreed in the partnership between UN-Habitat and the Songyang County People’s Government to further promote effective innovations to foster sustainable rural development and strengthen urban–rural linkages. The organisation behind the Forum on Urban–Rural Linkages in Songyang County is one of the key instruments for demonstrating this collaboration, making it an ideal platform to showcase urban–rural linkages in practice.

Looking ahead

Our world is an interconnected place with people sharing similar aspirations for hope and progress. Global agreements, policies, frameworks and agendas are ineffective if they fail to improve human living conditions and protect our environment. Songyang County has forged a path towards improving the quality of life for all its residents. The government's goals have been made possible through visionary leadership within its various tiers, partnerships, and the commitment and engagement of its citizens towards rebuilding their communities. Songyang County has the potential to continue inspiring many other communities by demonstrating the possibilities and potentials of rural development and revitalisation practices. Sustaining such efforts and scaling these practices to other contexts is a work in progress.

Eduard Kögel

Adapting Tradition for Contemporary Expression

The architect Xu Tiantian commutes regularly from the office she runs in the capital Beijing to Songyang County in the province of Zhejiang. But it is not just the distance of some 1,500 kilometres and the differing lifestyles in town and country that have to be bridged here. The question of what architecture in rural areas looks like today and what aesthetic qualities it must have needs to be considered from different perspectives, because the local population also have ideas about how they imagine their environment and their buildings to be. When asked their opinion, off-guard, they will most likely answer that the shape of the old village temple or a glittering façade from the big city would be good models for a new community centre. If the architect disagrees, they will have to convince their customers, which is more difficult with words than with models to look at. In Songyang County, Xu Tiantian uses a range of strategies to do justice to the respective construction task and the local context. Large new infrastructures are treated differently from buildings that fit into village or landscape neighbourhoods or those that only need repair.

The vernacular architecture of rural regions worldwide is defined by local conditions. In addition to available materials, craftsmanship and tradition, the form and scale of the buildings are determined by their functions, uses and available tools. Thus, one- to two-storey buildings that can be erected without heavy technical equipment are the norm. In the case of Songyang County, the traditional architecture in the region's villages often has an internal wooden construction enclosed by an outer rammed earth wall. In one- or two-storey buildings, the wooden construction supports the ceilings and the roof, and follows the traditional specifications in which the wooden parts are a post-and-beam construction composed of modular parts. Therefore, the proportions are bound to the possibilities of the material. The size of the village buildings could only be varied to a limited extent or, if more space was needed, another building had to be erected next to the existing one. This principle resulted in a clustered building typology that still exists today in rural areas in many variations. This typology can be found all over the world, especially where pre-industrial technology dominates. As a result, unique building traditions are to be found on almost every continent, but they are threatened by the onset of industrialisation and globalisation.

Contemporary with local characteristics

Around 1913, the Austrian architect Adolf Loos, who had long been seen as a marginal figure of European modernism, wrote about building in rural areas.[1] For him, modernism had nothing to do with form, but with a people's culture. He wrote "modern is always the economical material" and argued that in a forested area one has to build with wood, whereas in an area with limestone one has to build with limestone. For him, it only made sense to change the local building culture if it resulted in a fundamental improvement. Otherwise, architecture should use the existing know-how of local craftspeople and improve in small steps.[2]

The same attitude shaped Chinese craftsmanship for centuries before the collapse of industrialisation brought new materials and new opportunities to rural areas. The modular order, which shaped not only architecture but also the entire concept of creativity, is almost completely lost today.[3] Originally, the conceptual approach was important, but was given an individual touch by craftsmanship. Nature as a model – in which each tree, for example, has many thousands of leaves, all of which are similar but not the same – allowed maximum integration in the location. In this way, a more uniform architecture could be created, which, through adaptation, produced variations in the topography that are nevertheless committed to the same principles.

In Songyang, the traditional building technique with its modular order, both in construction and in spatial positioning, was preserved well into the twentieth century. Today, most villages are reshaped with contemporary buildings, whose reinforced concrete frame constructions, brick walls and tiled façades are reminiscent of their predecessors only in abstract decorations. In Songyang, these new buildings in the villages are often right next to neglected traditional houses and illustrate above all that the local population is looking for a contemporary solution with modern amenities.
A convincing argument for how upgrading of traditional buildings with new technical infrastructure and a contemporary approach can be successful requires a lot of patience and persuasiveness.

1
Adolf Loos, "Regeln für den, der in den Bergen baut" [Rules for those building in the mountains], published in Franz Glück (ed.), *Adolf Loos: Sämtliche Schriften*, Vol. 2 (Vienna, 1962), pp. 329–30.

2
Kurt Lustenberger, "Modern is Always the Sparing. On Three Rural Buildings by Adolf Loos", in *Daidados* Nr. 32, 15 June 1989, pp. 52–59.

3
Lothar Ledderose, *Ten Thousand Thinks. Module and Mass Production in Chinese Art* (Princeton, 2000), pp. 5–7.

The art of relation

Xu Tiantian speaks of acupuncture when explaining her method of interventions in an existing setting. As with traditional Chinese medicine, the aim is to stimulate regeneration in the vicinity of the injection site – or the place of intervention. But there is no single architectural language that makes her projects immediately identifiable. Depending on the situation and the programme, ideas can be found that provide a solution appropriate to the construction task based on the local context. One aspect is the repair of existing buildings or landscapes. Here, the new is integrated, as in the *Pingtian Village Centre* (p. 60), or it transforms an existing infrastructure such as the *Shimen Bridge* (p. 128), which follows the historical principle of covered bridges, but with new forms. Existing workshops such as the *Camellia Oil Workshop* (p. 150) have been renovated using historical building techniques, making it difficult for the layperson to distinguish the new from the old.

A second approach is based on using local techniques and materials to give new functions a contemporary form. *The Brown Sugar Factory* (p. 72) is a hybrid building at the entrance to the village, underlining its importance for the local population, with a transparent ground floor and industrial aesthetics. There are no references to traditional forms or decorations. The meaning is defined solely by its function as workshop and cultural centre. The same holds true for the *Wang Jing Memorial Hall* (p. 140), *Tofu Factory* (p. 194) or Madao Social Housing projects, each developing from the situational context and ingeniously inscribing itself into the urban structure. The local materiality and function combine to form the aesthetic expression of an elegant rusticity, which takes the respective conditions into account through its structure.

In China, the representation of nature in the garden is inconceivable without pavilions. From time immemorial, the pavilion has served as a platform for contemplation in the midst of a man-made composition of plants and stones dealing with literary themes. In traditional gardens, calligraphic inscriptions from past writers on walls or on stones encourage memory to be associated with current challenges. In the river landscape of Songyang, the pavilions of Xu Tiantian with their artistic installations are reference points where visitors can combine movement in fresh air with the experience of an agricultural environment. Here, agricultural production becomes a visual object stimulating the urban visitors with the fundamental issue of how to deal with the environment. These new pavilions do not primarily focus on the materiality of the building but instead reflect into the larger landscape with small architectural interventions. The surrounding area thus becomes a garden where agricultural production is represented.

Projects such as the *Dushan Leisure Centre* (p. 182) or the *Water Conservancy Centre* (p. 206) are new in their use and larger in their dimensions than the historical building types in rural areas. Here we come back to Adolf Loos' insight mentioned above. The local building culture can be changed if it makes sense in terms of content and if there are no local models. However, we must also pay attention here. What proportions can a building take in the respective context? How should it be structured, and which architectural concept is appropriate? Like the above-mentioned tree with its thousands of individual leaves, the building mass must be added to a composition which, while fulfilling its functions, respects the modular nature of the other individual parts in its proportions. Or to put it in the words of the British architect and urban designer Gordon Cullen: "[…] the aim is not to dictate the shape of the town or environment, but is a modest one: simply to *manipulate within the tolerances*".[4]

In all the variants of the architectural production of Xu Tiantian described here, the focus is on the very Chinese idea of modular composition, which is echoed both in the urban framework and in the architectural detail. The Korean philosopher Byung-Chul Han put it succinctly: "The guiding principle for modular production is not the idea of originality or uniqueness, but reproducibility. Their purpose is not to create a unique, original object, but to mass produce it, which allows variations and modulations." [5]

But it is also about the smallest possible intervention, illustrated perfectly by a project such as the *Bamboo Theatre* (p. 54). A plant becomes architecture and renews itself, so that only human

4
Gordon Cullen, *The Concise Townscape* (London, 1978), p. 8.

5
Byung-Chul Han, *Shanzhai. Dekonstruktion auf Chinesisch* (Berlin, 2011), p. 71.

manipulation is needed to create a meaningful social space. The work of Xu Tiantian in Songyang is significant far beyond the region and the country, because the results show that even with few means, an expanded aesthetic meaning can be created.

Dushan Leisure Centre

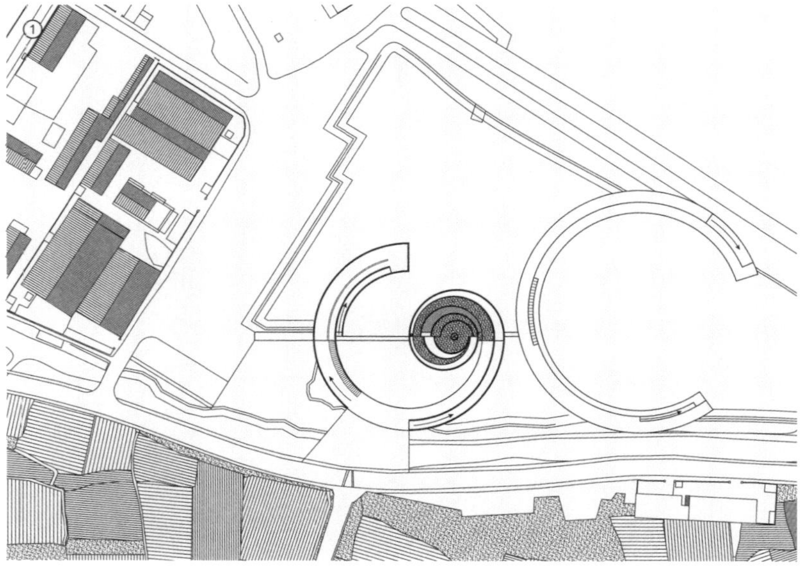

Dushan Mountain, Silingxia Village 2018

The steep slopes of Dushan Mountain with its pagoda on top mark the entrance to the urban centre of Songyang County. At the foot of the mountain, the leisure centre is located in a triangular pool connected to the nearby Songyin River. The centre is laid out as a spiral and is entered via a diagonal bridge. Various functions for exhibitions, services or sports are accommodated in segments of the spiral. The circular core of the centre has two storeys and can be accessed over ramps on the inside and outside. The homogeneous, darkly stained wood of the structure contrasts with the extensive glazing.

Visitors experience the architecture by circling through the space. In the interior, attention is guided from the inside to the outside by the slowly changing transparency of the glazing. In the open air, the ramps provide a lookout over the landscape. With each movement, the attention thus shifts between near and far or vice versa. Visitors can either focus on the landscape context with the mountain or concentrate on the interior garden and exhibition spaces.

The outward swinging "arm" of the spiral houses training facilities for water sports enthusiasts. Rowing machines are installed in a pool at the end of the space, allowing a view of the landscape. A circular bridge segment, where visitors can rent boats, connects both banks and the pavilion in the water.

Client: Songyang Tourism Development Co., Ltd.

① Site plan
② Axonometric drawing
1 roof layer; 2 first floor, wooden structure; 3 ground floor, wooden structure; 4 first floor; 5 ground floor; 6 tasting hall
③ Detail section façade
④+⑤ Side elevation

②

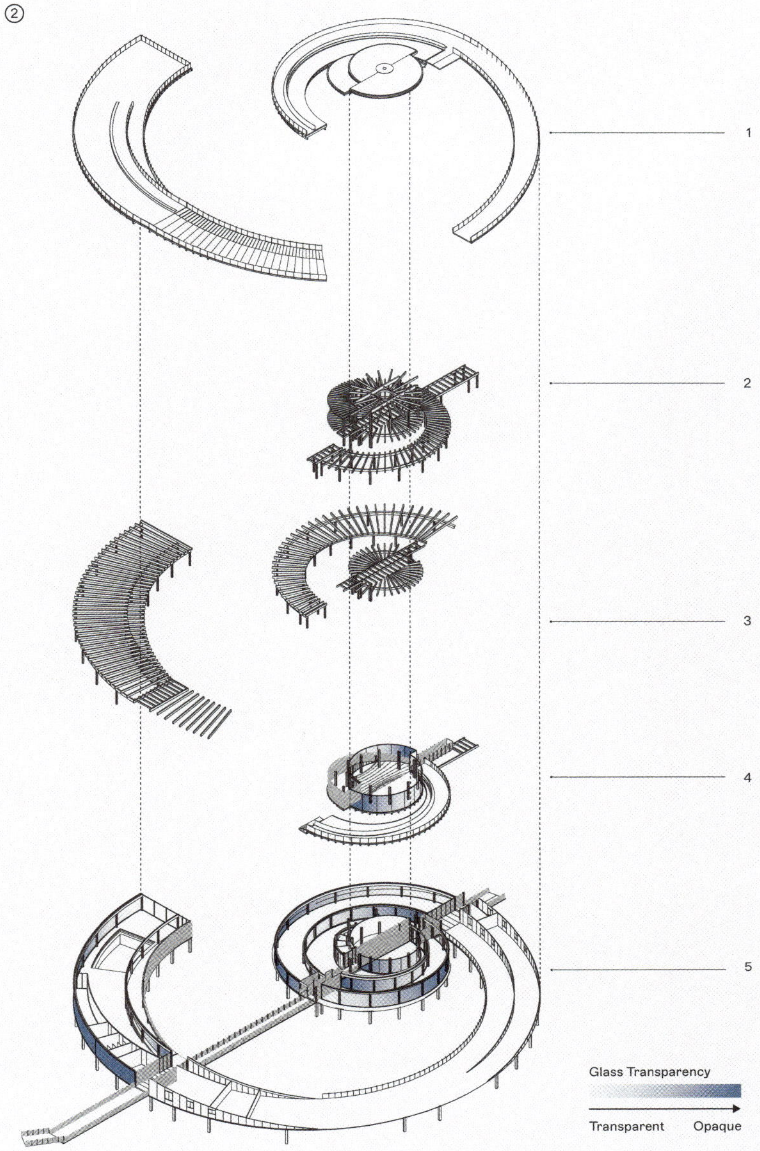

③

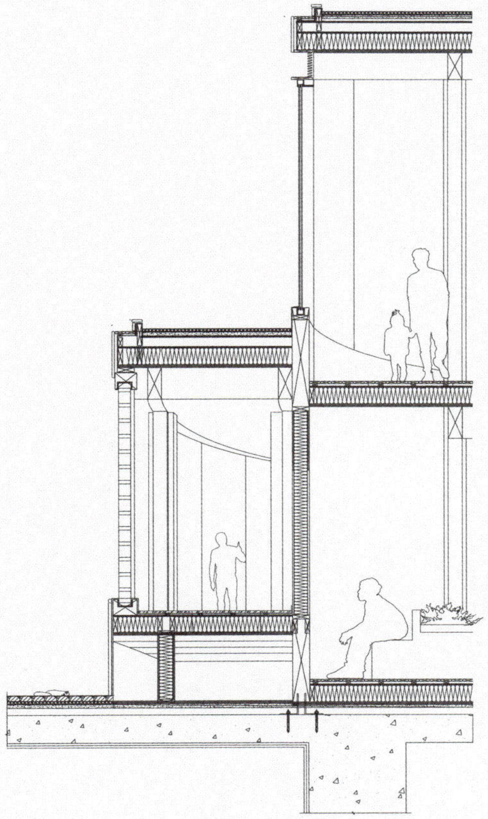

④

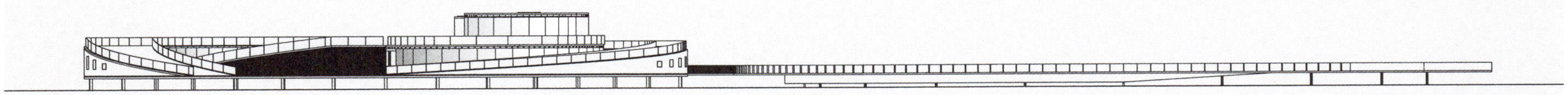

⑤

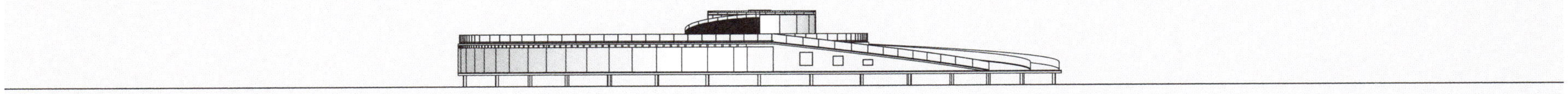

Tofu Factory

Caizhai Village, Datongba Town, Songyang 2018

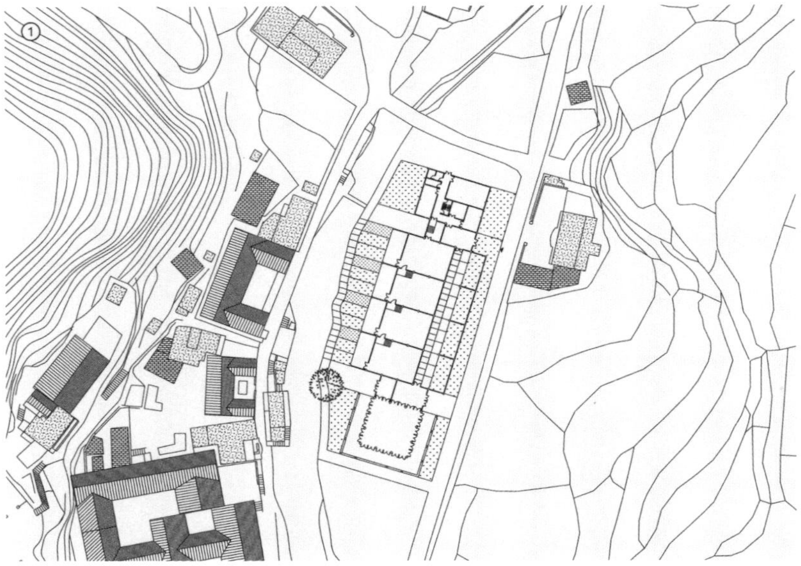

In the southern part of Songyang County, the village of Caizhai lies in a mountainous landscape. The village has been built over the last 200 years along a small river and has long been known for its excellent tofu production. Traditionally, the families worked in their own small workshops, which did not meet today's food standards for the sale of the products. A village joint venture was established to build a tofu factory, which the families can enter as shareholders, thus gaining access to an expanded market that provides them with a higher income. The building site of the new tofu factory is located at the entrance to the village, making it a visible sign of a new era.

Tofu is made from white soybeans processed into soy milk. The resulting soy curd is dehydrated and pressed into blocks to be further processed in various ways. These processes require different work steps, which are carried out in separate rooms of the factory to achieve hygiene standards for sale.

The tofu factory follows a slight slope in six stages, each with its own unit, from north to south: beginning with the preparation rooms, followed by the soy milk production hall, the cooking department, the deep-frying hall, the drying department and finally the tasting hall for visitors at the entrance to the village. The whole complex is a prefabricated contemporary wooden construction, which has similarities to the traditional mortise and tenon wooden construction of the old village houses.

The transparent workshop stands in contrast to the rammed earth walls in the village, although an allusion to traditional building methods can be seen in the construction. The population easily accepted this form of renewal, which references scale and materiality, but adapts function and technical equipment to present-day needs.

Client: Economic Cooperation Limited of Caizhai Village, Datongba Town

① Site plan
② Axonometric drawing
1 tasting hall; 2 drying hall; 3 deep-frying hall;
4 boiling hall; 5 milling hall; 6 preparation rooms
③ Section
④ Sectional perspective

②

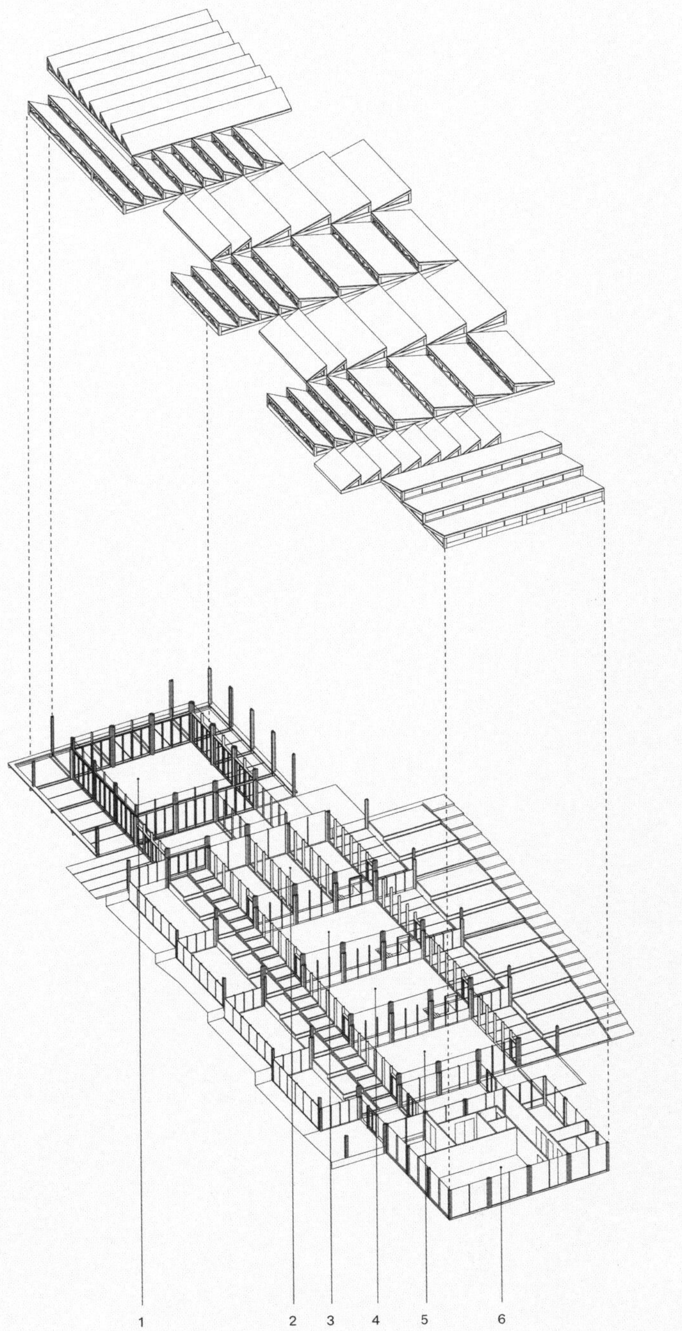

③

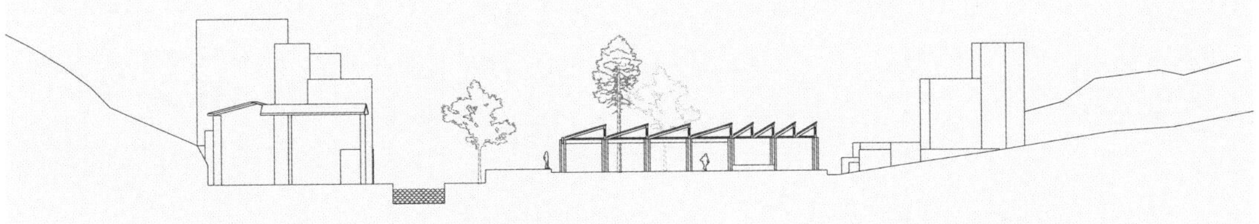

④

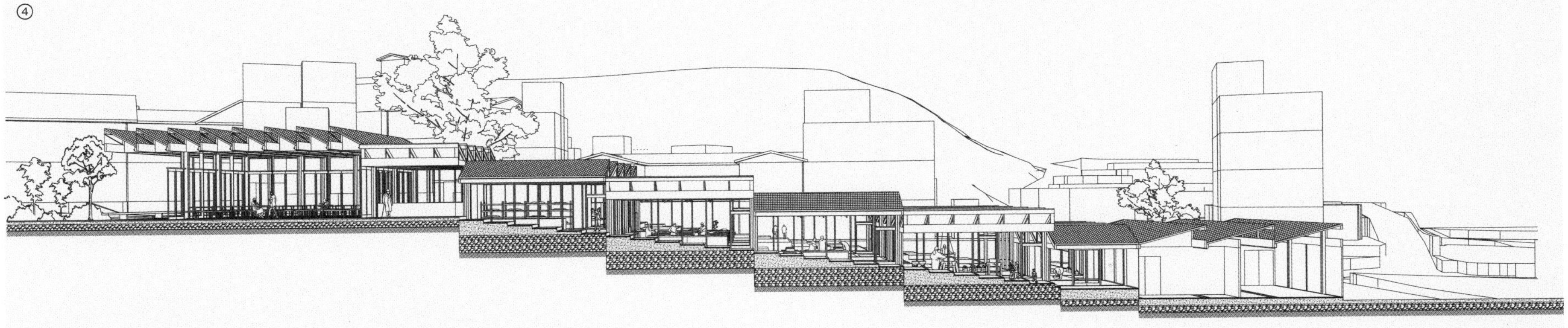

欢迎您

EXIT

EXIT

EXIT

Water Conservancy Centre

Baisha Lake Hydropower Station 2019

Client: River Dam, Dykes and Reservoir Management Department of Songyang County

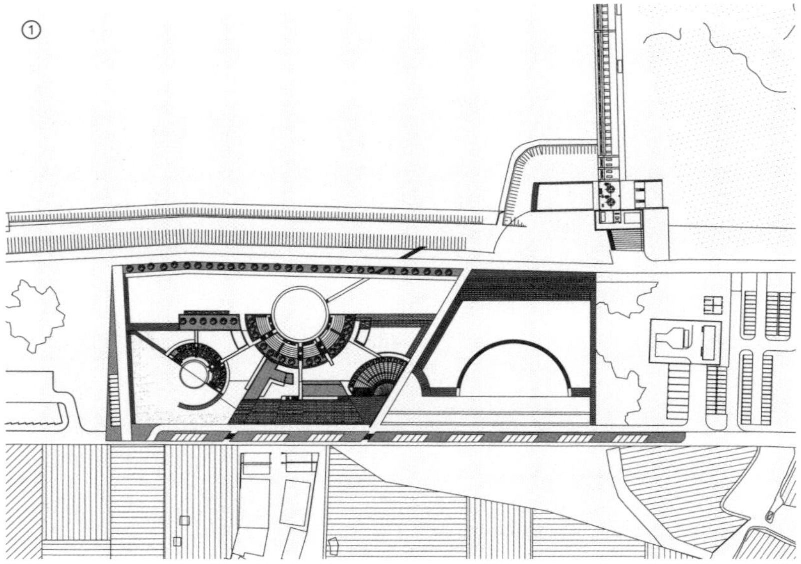

The Water Conservancy Centre for the district of Songyang is situated next to the Songyin River, in the countryside, outside the administrative centre of the district. The building houses two management departments for a future hydropower plant and a monitoring centre for water management, as well as a canteen and archives. The construction programme is embedded in a water park that combines public attraction with educational content.

The three main buildings are made up of circular segments and have a roof that is designed as an amphitheatre inviting visitors to take part in outdoor activities. The other roofs of the buildings are planted with trees that connect with the green scenery of the rural surroundings.

The programmatic part links the archive to the exhibition area, where the local history of water regulation is shown. On request, the observation centre opens to local school classes or visitors so they can learn more about the subject. The canteen not only serves staff and visitors but also is used as a multimedia room for the younger generation. The individual building components are combined in the water park. Its open spaces contribute to the diversity of public learning spaces in this vital infrastructure.

The massive buildings with their homogeneous façades made of worked stone and the paths across the water made of the same material stand like monoliths in the aquatic park landscape. The paths support a diverse relationship between the surrounding landscape and the different areas of the site. The Water Conservancy Centre is part of an overall learning landscape along the river, which runs through the whole Songyin valley.

① Site plan
② Axonometric drawing
③+④ Section

②

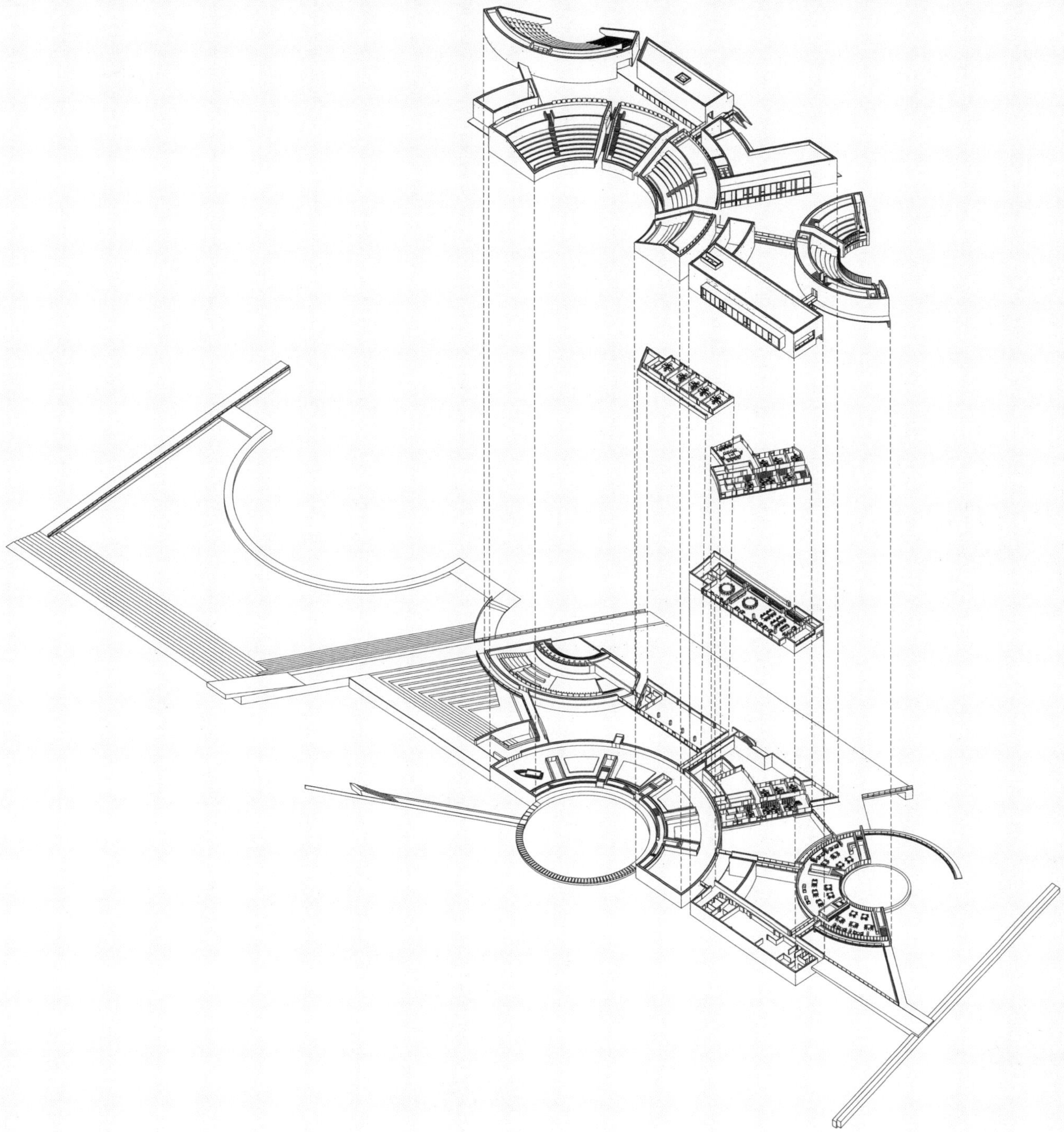

③

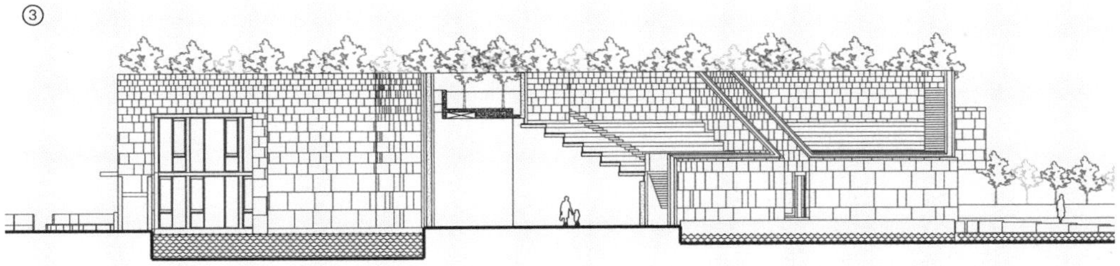

④

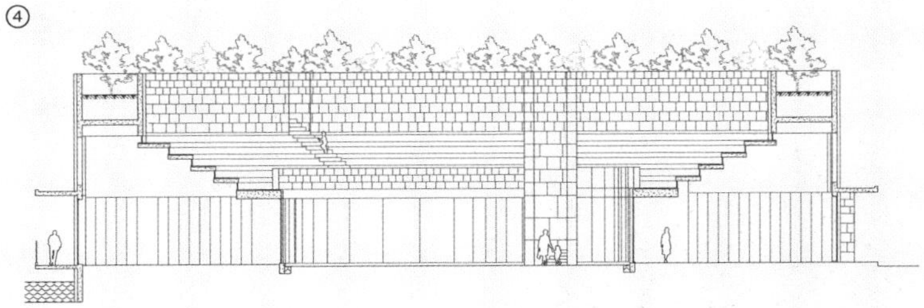

松阳水系
WATER SYSTEM OF
SONGYANG COUNTY

Rice Wine Factory

Shantou Village, Datongba Town 2019

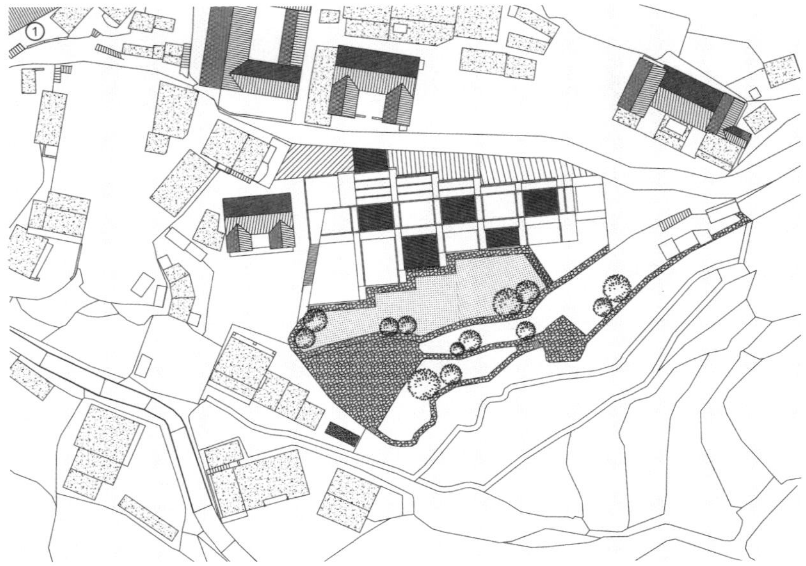

The Rice Wine Factory is located at the edge of the village on an irregular site. In the background lie the heterogeneous buildings of the village, while in the foreground the agricultural landscape reaches right up to the new building. The architect responded to the irregular shape of the building site with a volume stepped on both sides, which blends well into the proportions of the village.

Rice wine is a traditional drink with up to 25 per cent alcohol content. During production, the rice must be fermented and distilled, and the rice starch is processed into sugar. The production of rice wine is a complex process requiring some hyperclean rooms. If a show workshop is to be created that also serves as a tourist attraction, the paths of production and those of visitors must be strictly separated.

The access corridor for employees, from which the various production rooms are entered, runs through the middle of the workshop. Visitors are led from the village side into a separate corridor, which allows a view of the production through large glass panels. The storerooms for the rice wine in the basement are accessible by elevator. The lounges and wine-tasting rooms for visitors are located on the upper floor and reached via stairs. The vaulted ceilings of the rooms give the impression of old wine cellars. The building has a structure of exposed concrete, whilst the openings are transparently connected to the surroundings by a wall of staggered red bricks.

The floor surfaces are made of red bricks divided by ribbons of exposed concrete. The reduction to basic materials, used without further refinement, and the simple, arched motif for the ceiling and openings give this factory a rustic expression that blends in well with the rural scenery.

Client: Economic Cooperation Limited of Shantou Village, Datongba Town

① Site plan
② Axonometric drawing
1 storage area; 2 lift; 3 wine cellar; 4 production area; 5 cleaning room; 6 wrapper room; 7 sterile room; 8 fermentation room; 9 locker room; 10 liquor storage; 11 steam generator; 12 tool room; 13 filling room; 14 blending room; 15 steam room; 16 storage yard; 17 visitors' passage; 18 sealing room; 19 recreation area; 20 rest room; 21 testing area
③ Ground floor plan
1 utility room; 2 yeast brewing room; 3 grain steeping room; 4 steaming room; 5 fermentation room; 6 wine storage; 7 jar sealing room; 8 packaging room; 9 dishwashing room
④ Sectional perspective

②

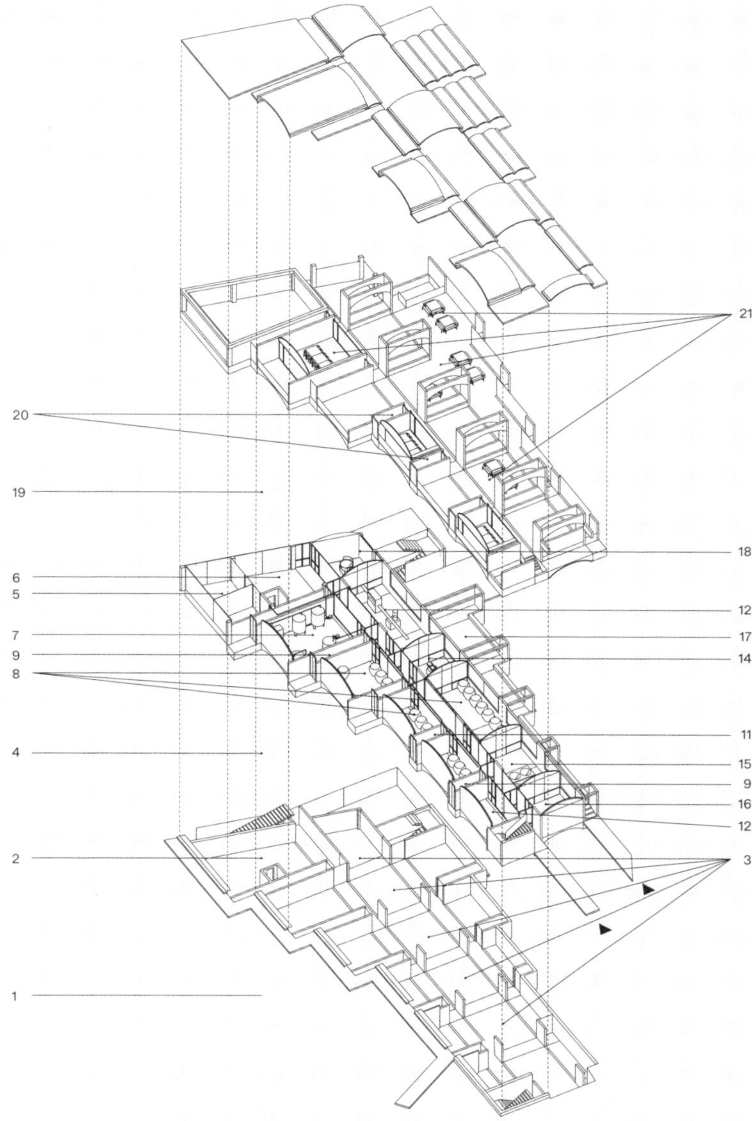

③

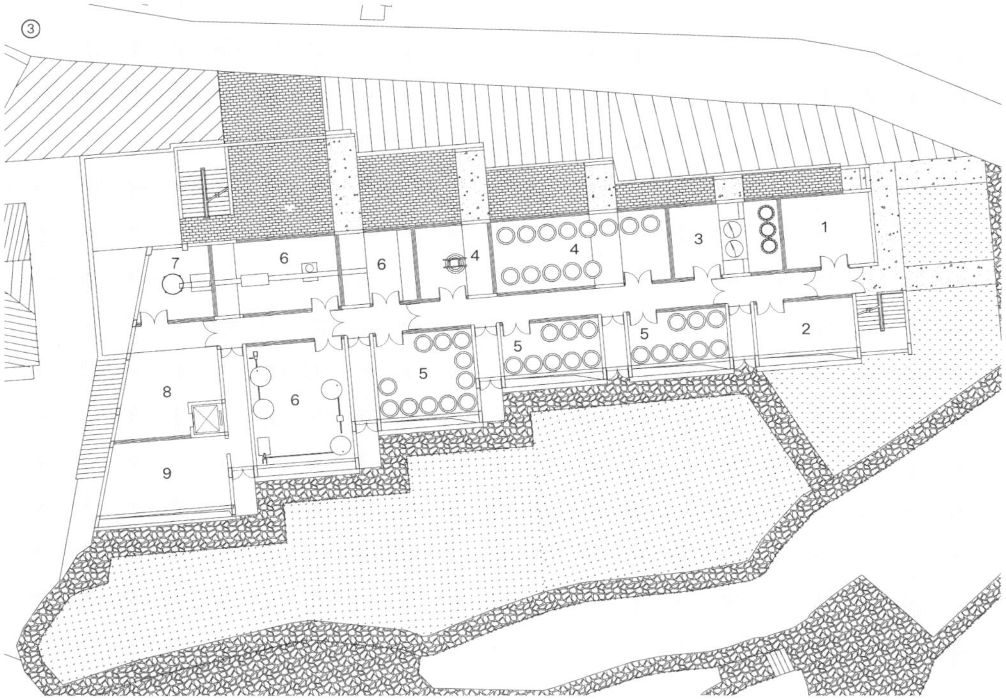

④

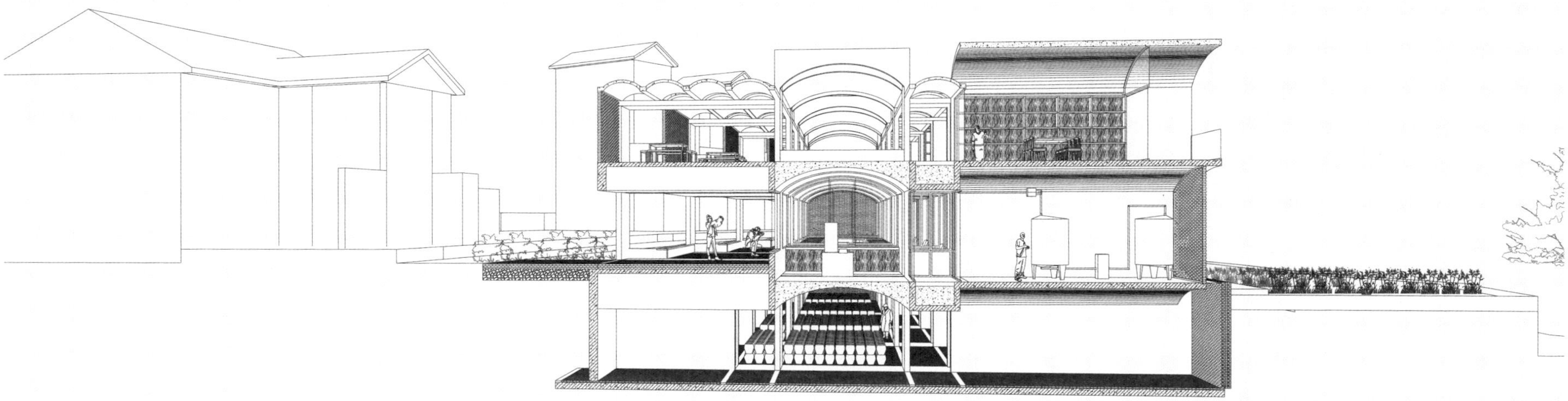

Maritime Museum

Qingtian Madao, Songyang County Seat 2019

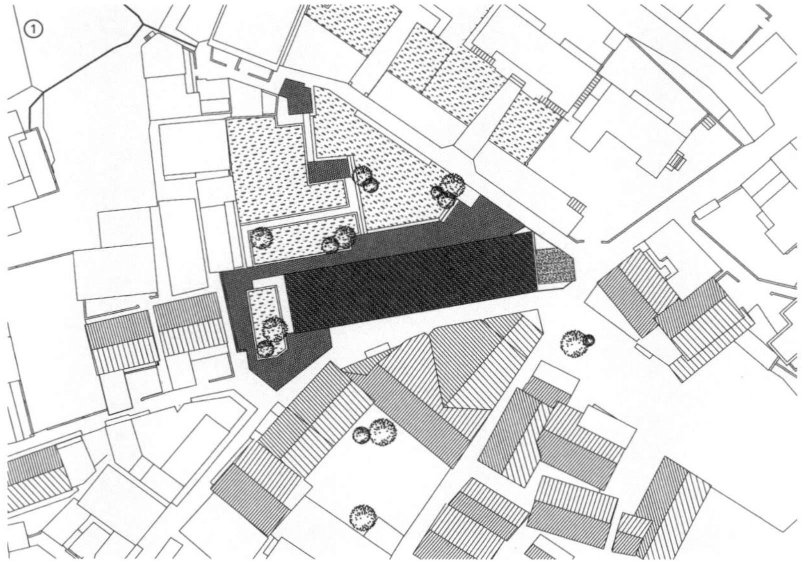

For a long time, because of its mountainous topography, the region of Songyang was only accessible by small roads and paths. This is why the waterways were very important for the transport of goods until the beginning of the twentieth century.

The Maritime Museum is located in the Qingtian Madao district between the Songyin and Nanming rivers in the county seat. The shipyard workers used to live in this area. The building preserves the original qualities of the shipyards and warehouses and expands them with workshops and exhibition spaces. In the neighbourhood to the south, there are narrow buildings with alleys, while to the north there is a bamboo garden.

Like a telescope, this linear museum building extends along the southern edge of the plot and steps down from three floors to one. The front elevations of each floor are glazed and allow plenty of daylight into the interior. Where the museum meets the street, the new building connects with a polygonal three-storey existing building in which smaller-scale uses are accommodated.

From the glazed rear entrance, visitors enter an elongated exhibition room, whose front wall has a diagonal staircase leading to the second floor. Another staircase leads to the third level, which is glazed on its gable side and merges into the existing building. The side to the alley has almost no openings. The gallery rooms are used for exhibitions of the maritime history and culture of the region. The old and new parts are separated by a two-storey patio, which is roofed over on the third floor. The material used for the inner and outer walls is the homogeneous grey brick of the region, integrating the museum into the existing neighbourhood. The reduction to a few local materials allows spatial clarity in which the effect of the exhibits can unfold.

Client: Ming-Cheng Conservation, Application and Development Cooperation Ltd. of Songyang County

① Site plan
② Axonometric drawing
③ Side elevation
④+⑤ Sectional perspective

②

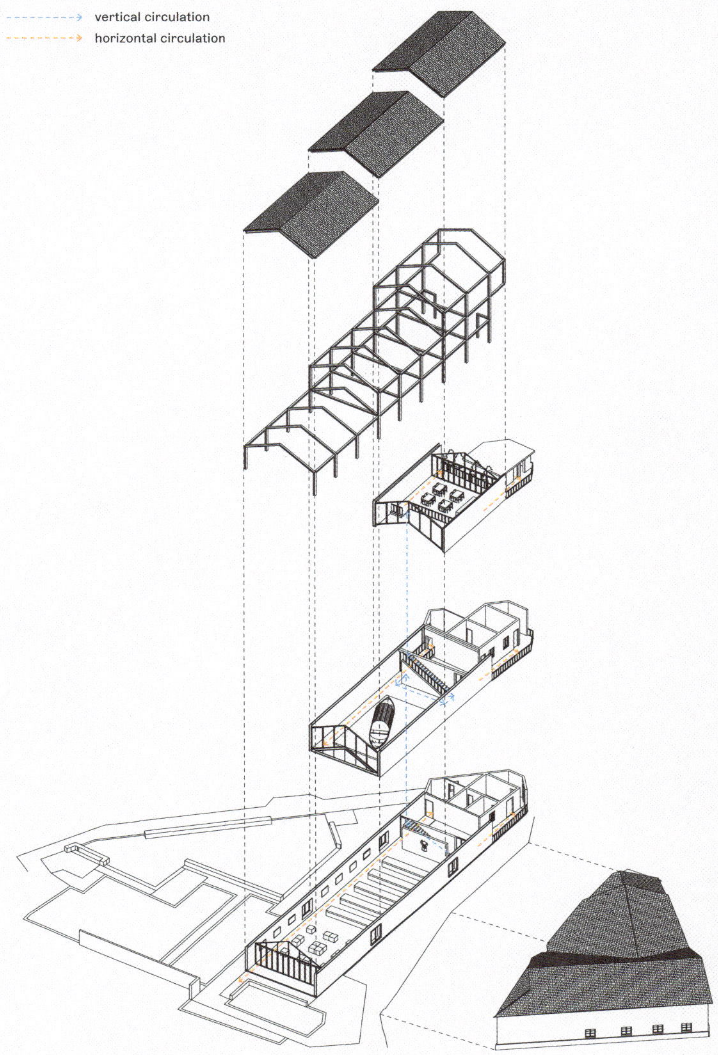

③

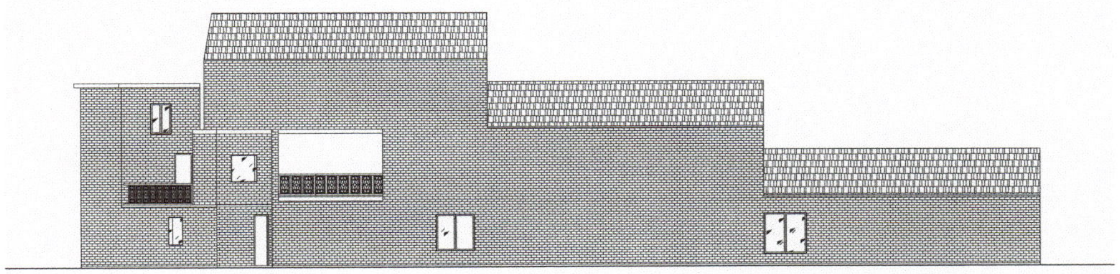

④

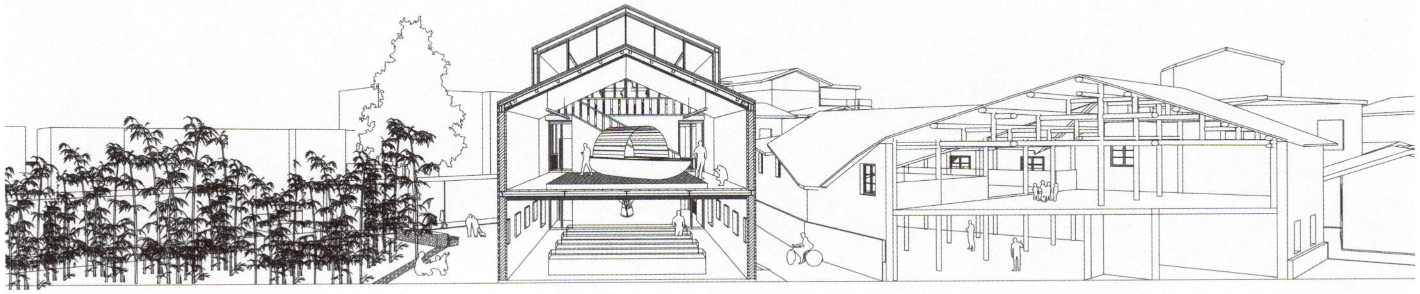

⑤

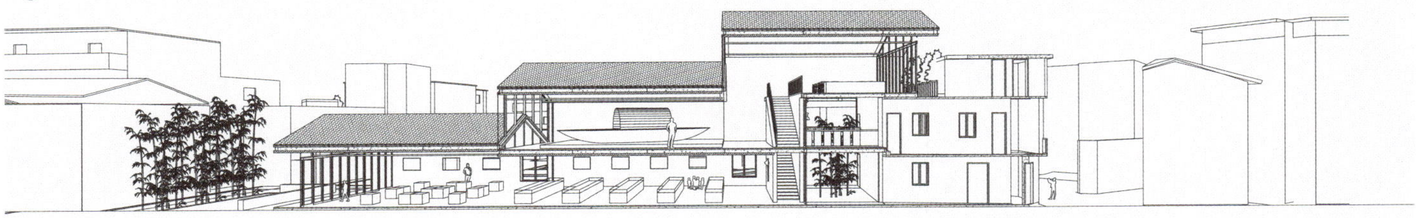

Village Housing & Homestay Cooperative

Shangtian Village 2020

Client: Economic Cooperative of Shangtian Village

①

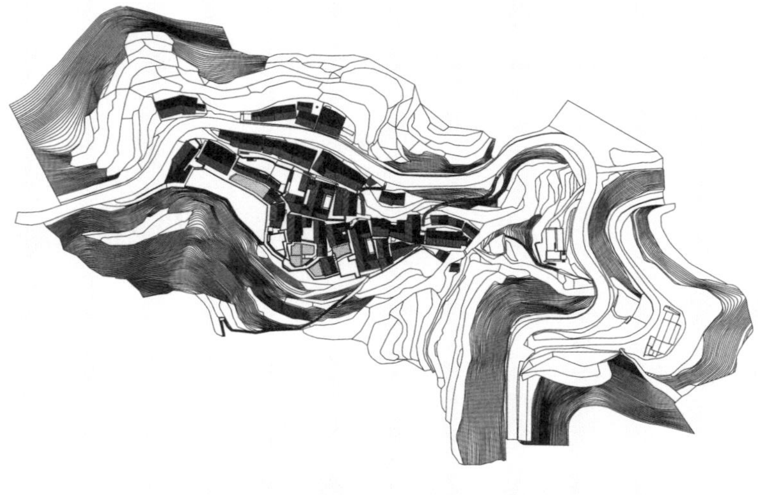

Shangtian is a typical mountain village with a 600-year-old history, but in recent years it has been confronted with a common dilemma: the younger generation moved to the cities and many houses stood empty and were finally abandoned.

With its ancient heritage of rammed earth buildings and its scenic beauty, Shangtian offers significant values and potential for rural tourism. Most of the vacant houses were preserved and converted into homestay accommodations and other leisure facilities. The newly founded collective business is owned by the village community and financed by both the villagers and the local government. The villagers contributed their land and became shareholders. Those who stay in the village can be employed in the new business. A total of 30 rooms were built for visitors, which can generate a gross annual income of three million RMB (approximately 390,000 euro). This is a pioneering experimental cooperative system that preserves the ownership and potential value of the village and prevents rip-offs or inequality caused by urban investment.

For the planning and design Xu Tiantian followed her ideas of "minimal intervention" in order to combine the rural character with necessary new infrastructures. The highlights of the area, like trees and wells, are integrated along a new sewerage system. The natural beauty of the landscape and the houses built with local materials perfectly match the expectations of tourists from the city, but the new village cooperative is of equal importance. The village can only survive in the market as a community. So three factors have come together here: a new legal form of business, an architect who gets the maximum out of the local potential with minimal interventions, and visitors who appreciate the resulting quality.

① Site plan
② Axonometric drawing restaurant
③ Topography and function
1 bathroom; 2 reception; 3 restaurant; 4 guest rooms; 5 communal kitchen; 6 communal buildings; 7 local dwellings; 8 workshops
④ Sectional perspective restaurant

②

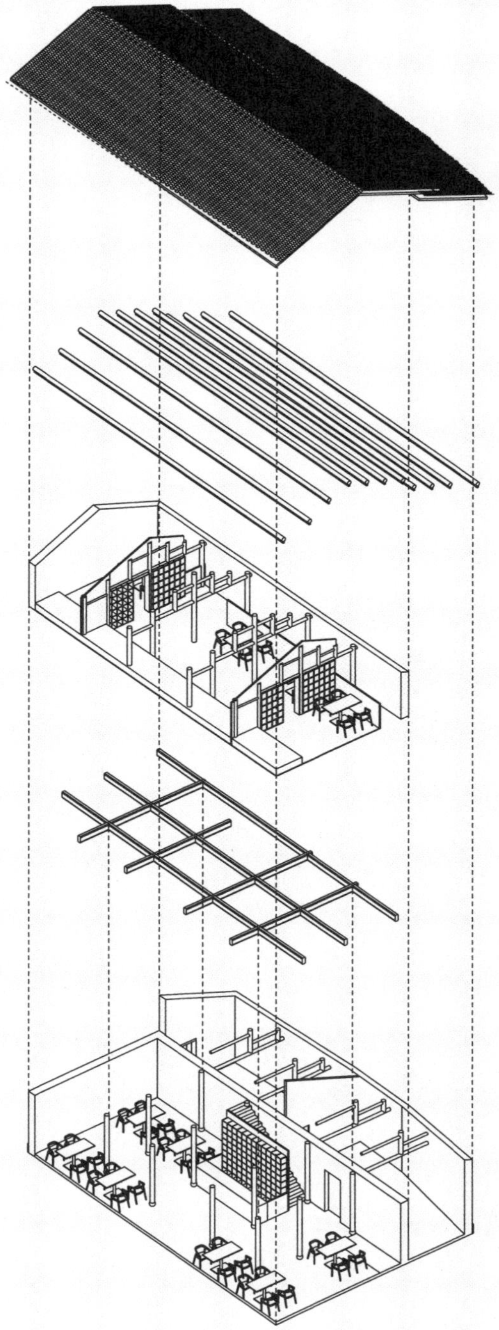

③

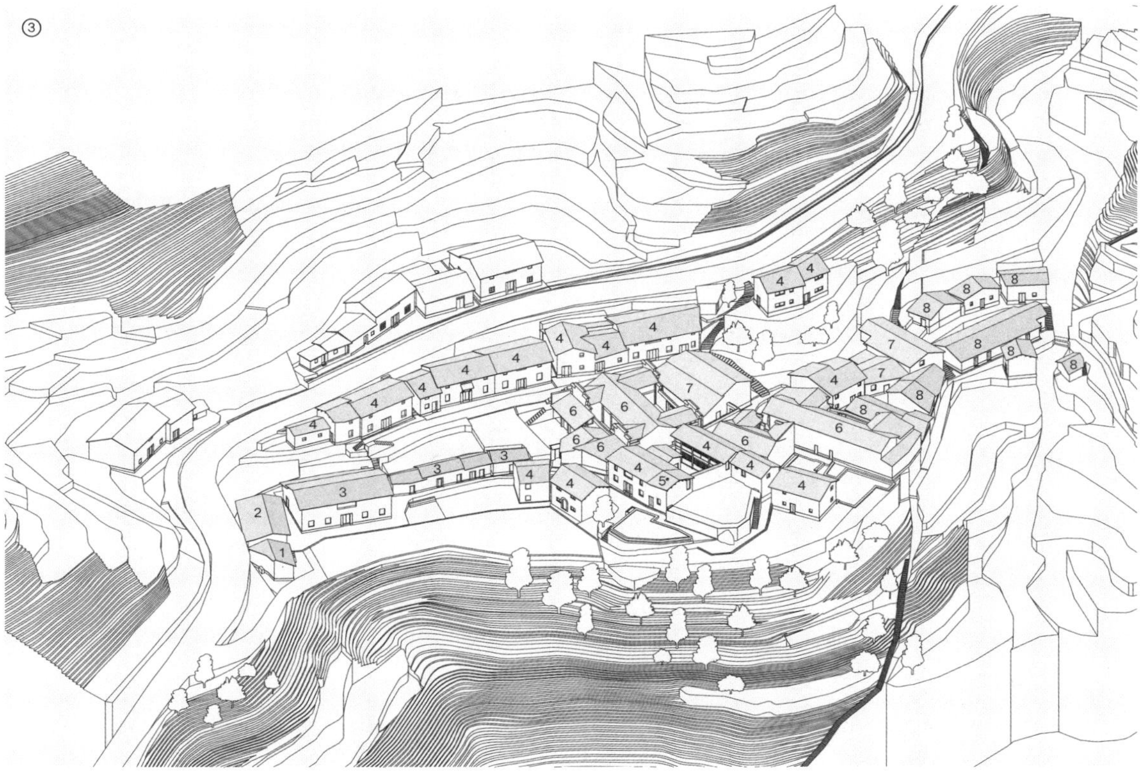

④

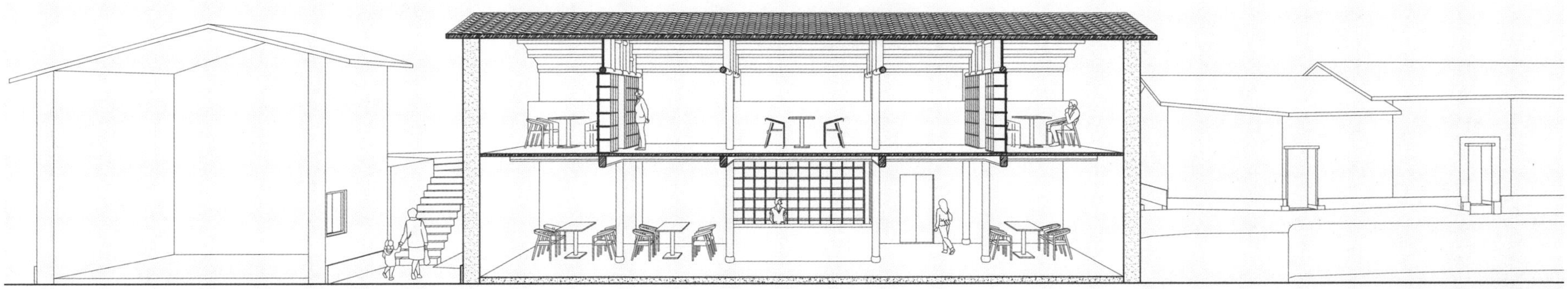

安全出口
EXIT

Eduard Kögel

The Future Is Now

Can architecture influence the sustainable revitalisation of rural areas?

As this book is being compiled, many new projects by DnA in Songyang are in the making. Some are in planning, some are under construction and some will already be completed by the time the first readers hold this publication in their hands. Therefore, a few important issues regarding new and upcoming projects are highlighted here, since they will continue to help to shape the future of the region.

Firstly, there are some questions regarding rural development in Songyang: Who benefits from all these small-scale architectural projects? What role do the inhabitants play? Is it enough to bring people back from the cities to the countryside, or are strategies needed that put the common good first? If the development is seen as positive by investors from the big city, completely new desires arise, which can easily lead to an exploitation of rural people and potentials. How do politicians and planners react to this? Are there projects that respond to this challenge? And finally: Can this strategy be transferred to other places in China? Or can it even be used in other countries and cultures to stimulate positive development there? The special thing about Songyang is that architecture plays an important role in the region and that the architect Xu Tiantian tries to find new solutions based on locally existing specifications. Not only has the local population accepted these solutions, but the new buildings also represent a freshly reawakened pride in rural life. So, what are the ingredients needed to influence the sustainable success of rural revitalisation with architecture?

Party Secretary Wang Jun said at a UN conference in Nairobi in May 2019: “We have adopted tourism as an important driving force for economic development on the county level and promoted the county’s standardised production base for green food, leisure, the rural museum and folk festivals on all county levels.” According to Wang “almost 120 villages in the county have implanted new forms of private enterprises, such as bed and breakfast accommodations, farmhouses, ecological agriculture, and cultural industries”.[1] The same newspaper report also claims that the number of tourists has increased significantly within two years. It is therefore understandable that many small projects have been started in the tourism sector. However, this boom needs

1
Edith Mutethya, “Songyang’s architectural acupunctures impress experts”, *chinadaily.com.cn*, updated 29.05.2019: http://www.chinadaily.com.cn/a/201905/29/WS5cee481ba3104842260be832g.html (accessed 29.1.2020).

a sustainable infrastructure that not only meets the needs of visitors, but also improves inhabitants' lives.

Investments from the private sector are also necessary, coming from companies that know exactly what is of interest to the urban middle class. Visitors, who are potentially willing to spend money, expect certain amenities and an intact environment that satisfies their need for recreation and wellness. This does not fit together with old people living in poor conditions in the villages of a mountainous hinterland. For decades they have survived self-sufficiently here since their children migrated to the city. The needs of these local villagers must be taken into account in order to initiate a development that will sustainably reach different groups of the population.

New addition to the Silk Farming Factory.

Against the background of positive development in the tourism sector it is not surprising that some of Xu Tiantian's new projects are located in this field. For instance, the Silk Farming Workshop in Shiwuli village is being implemented by turning an existing building into an "edutainment" facility for visitors. The village has a long history of sericulture, which has slowly been diminishing since the seventies. However, the landscape around the village is still dominated by mulberry trees and is thus a good starting point to introduce visitors to the culture of silk production. Together with the oil workshop, the sugar workshop, the tofu and rice wine production facilities, and a further workshop for pottery (in planning), such economic opportunities on a regional scale are being created that can complement one another. Each of the participating villages tries to use its potential in a new way and to stimulate economic growth with the help of tourism while also harnessing the knowledge of the old people.

The Dalutan Blueberry Pavilion next to Songyin River.

A number of small pavilions and other facilities along the Songyin River were created, like pearls on a necklace, as places in which to inform passing hikers and cyclists about local products such as tea or tree resin. One pavilion, due to be completed in the spring of 2020, focuses on the processing of blueberries, which have been grown locally for some time. The *Dalutan Blueberry Pavilion* rises above the surrounding linear fields and offers a panoramic view across the agricultural landscape. The processing of the blueberries takes place in a show workstation, allowing the visitors insights into production processes. The pavilion is three storeys high and is entered directly from the street at the middle storey. The lower floor houses the sanitary rooms and work facilities. Through a large opening, visitors can view the work being done from the middle floor. On the top floor there is a large public and a smaller private tea room as well as viewing platforms on both sides. Above the tea rooms, an asymmetrical butterfly roof surrounds the patio, connecting the ground floor with the first floor via a staircase planted with trees.

Not far from Dushan Mountain – a natural landmark in the middle of the valley – is the *Qinglongyan Visitors' Lounge*, a viewing platform and rest area, which is also scheduled for completion in the spring of 2020. It is a small square box with a simple steel construction and stands next to the Songyin River. It is reached from the road via an elevated path. On the lower floor there is open access to the pond, which can be reached via a wide staircase. The ground floor houses a shop with external stairs to the left and right leading to a tea room on the first floor. The façades between the restrained steel construction are glazed all around. Another external staircase leads to the roof, where a stepped, open seating area offers a view of the agricultural plain and the panoramic mountain landscape behind it.

Qingyonglan Visitors' Lounge allows a view across the river landscape.

In addition to tapping the natural and cultural potential for tourism infrastructure and thus for new economic opportunities, investments must also be made where the financial and social possibilities of the people from the valley are limited. Rapidly rising housing prices are already affecting the developing rural areas. It is therefore inevitable that there will be a need to build social housing to adequately accommodate the economically disadvantaged members of society.

The town of Qingtian Madao lies between the Nanming and Songyin rivers in Songyang. Until the beginning of the twentieth century, the land here was regularly flooded and only became useable after the construction of a dam. Today, a plan for new low-cost social housing on this land is part of the redevelopment plan for the entire district. The formerly dense, semi-rural development with small ponds and public alleys is being replaced by a high-rise quarter, which is currently under construction.

The buildings for Madao Social Housing mediate in their height development between the adjacent existing buildings.

The density and orientation of the 430 planned apartments is predetermined by both building regulations and community participation, as well as by the legally stipulated minimal solar radiation for each unit. In order to achieve the required density, modern high-rise buildings were an unavoidable solution. Xu Tiantian uses her ten new 8- to 15-storey buildings to connect the traditional low houses on the west side to existing high-rise buildings on the east side of the plot. The ground floors of the new residential buildings will be open and the existing paths and alleys, as well as the small ponds, will be integrated into the landscape design. This will create a coherent park landscape running beneath the blocks that is also open to the wider neighbourhood.

The entire complex, with its communal landscape carpet below and stepped buildings that blend into the context like a mountain backdrop, creates a three-dimensional spatial image that corresponds with the mountain silhouette on the horizon. The organic interlocking of the design will serve as an antithesis to the homogeneous façades of the new buildings since, because of a very tight budget, the only variables will be the exterior spaces and the height staggering.

The plan shows how existing landscape structures were integrated into the new development.

In addition to the residential buildings described here, further projects are in planning or under construction. Most of them mainly serve the wider field of tourism. To date, a new village co-op and social housing are the only exceptions. If the entire development in Songyang is to become a sustainable model, additional effort will be needed in the long term to, for example, educate and provide additional training for the local population. There must be attractive offers for teachers too, so that the young do not leave the area. In addition, efforts need to be made to further open up the participation process and actively involve village communities in the shaping of their own living and working spaces. Other challenges also lie ahead in health care and in ecological forms of economy that will make small-scale agriculture more profitable in the region.

Those responsible are aware of the challenges and are searching for solutions. It is a case of, as former leader Deng Xiaoping put it during the economic opening of China: "cross[ing] the river while feeling for stones". In other words: just try it out and adjust if necessary.

Whether the Songyang strategies can work in other places depends on many factors. Natural and cultural resources play just as much a role as the willingness of the inhabitants to get involved in new things. Certainly, the idea of a new rural architecture and the economic potential for development will have to be adapted to real situations. How, for example, can one initiate a positive development by architectural means if the landscape is not as attractive or the region is difficult to reach?

Although the examples shown here are encouraging and have generated a positive echo worldwide, many questions remain unanswered. We will continue to observe the development and, of course, hope that it will serve as an example to other regions in China – and beyond – of how small architectural interventions can be used to bring hope back into village communities.

Biographies

Hans-Jürgen Commerell

Hans-Jürgen Commerell is a photographer, curator and publisher. He studied social and business communication at the University of the Arts in Berlin. As an architecture photographer, he has been published in international magazines and realised a number of books, such as *Kunstmuseum Bonn* and *The Jewish School Berlin* (both published by Wasmuth, 1994 and 1995 respectively) as well as *Clorindo Testa: Architect* (NAi, 2000). He has been director of Aedes Architecture Forum in Berlin together with its founder Kristin Feireiss since 1994. As a curator, he has contributed to numerous exhibitions in the field of architecture and urbanism for Aedes and in commission for other cultural institutions. During Kristin Feireiss' time at the Netherlands Architecture Institute from 1996 to 2001, Commerell diversified the programme of Aedes. In addition to monographic exhibitions, the focus has veered towards the city as social, cultural and political habitat. Aedes invites cities from all continents to present their various urban strategies. Since the turn of the millennium, he has been looking more closely into East Asian cultural space and established a continuous and intensive exchange with China. In 2009, Commerell conceptualised and established, together with Kristin Feireiss, the international Metropolitan Laboratory Aedes Network Campus Berlin (ANCB) in collaboration with international universities. ANCB complements the exhibition programme of Aedes as a cultural and public transdisciplinary discourse platform focusing on the interplay of societal and technological innovation.

Kristin Feireiss

Dr. h.c. Kristin Feireiss was born in Berlin. She studied art history and philosophy and is an architecture curator, author and publisher, as well as the founder (together with Helga Retzer, †1984) and director (together with Hans-Jürgen Commerell) of the Aedes Architecture Forum in Berlin, the first independent architecture gallery world-wide. Feireiss was Director of the Netherlands Architecture Institute (NAi) in Rotterdam and jury member of the Pritzker Architecture Prize. As Director of both the NAi and Aedes Architecture Forum, she has brought greater attention to urban transformation processes and carried out groundbreaking research in this area, accompanied by exhibitions, publications and symposia. Her most important concern, however, is to awaken interest in the broader public for architecture and urban design and to raise awareness for the fact that the built environment concerns everyone. Feireiss has edited numerous monographs and thematic volumes on architecture and the urban context.

Eduard Kögel

Eduard Kögel studied urban and landscape planning at the University of Kassel (GhK) and received his doctorate from the Bauhaus University in Weimar. From 1999 to 2004 he taught as Assistant Professor at the Technical University in Darmstadt in the department of Non-European Architecture and Urban Development. He has written widely on the history of architecture; his books include *The Chinese City* (Jovis, 2000) and *The Grand Documentation: Ernst Boerschmann and Religious Architecture in China* (De Gruyter, 2015) and *EXH Design. Swiss Quality – Chinese Speed* (Jovis, 2018). Kögel is also a research consultant and programme curator for ANCB The Aedes Metropolitan Laboratory, and has curated several exhibitions on contemporary Chinese architecture at the Aedes Architecture Forum in Berlin. Since 2006, he has curated the website chinese-architects.com. He teaches regularly at the Technical University Berlin and the Bauhaus University Weimar and is a member of the board of ski – stadtkultur international e.v. For over 20 years he has been intensively involved in cultural exchange between Europe and Asia.

Saskia Sassen

Saskia Sassen is the Robert S. Lynd Professor of Sociology at Columbia University and a member of its Committee on Global Thought, which she chaired from 2009 until 2015. She is a student of cities, immigration and states in the world economy, with inequality, gendering and digitisation being three key variables running though her work. Born in the Netherlands, she grew up in Argentina and Italy, studied in France, was raised in five languages, and began her professional life in the United States. She is the author, editor or co-editor of many books. Together, her authored books have been translated in over 20 languages. She has received many awards and honours, among them 20 honoris causa doctorates, multiple named lectures, the 2013 Principe de Asturias Award for Social Sciences, and election as a foreign member of the Royal Netherlands Academy of Arts and Sciences, and was made a Chevalier de l'Ordre des Arts et des Lettres by the French government. She regularly writes for general audience publications. Her comments have appeared in *The Guardian*, *The New York Times*, *Le Monde diplomatique*, *Le Monde*, *La Vanguardia*, *Clarín*, *Die Zeit*, *Newsweek* and *The Financial Times*, among others.

Remy Sietchiping

Remy Sietchiping is Chief of Policy, Legislation and Governance Section within the Urban Practices branch of UN-Habitat at its Headquarters in Nairobi, Kenya. He is currently working on national urban policies with spatial frameworks, legislation governance 'Urban Corridors' development, and 'Urban-Rural Linkages'. Sietchiping has coordinated global, regional and country projects and programmes in Africa, Asia and Latin America. He joined UN-Habitat in 2007 where he devoted his energy towards supporting land issues – in particular the Global Land Tool Network (GLTN). He later spearheaded work on the development and implementation of international guidelines on urban and territorial planning. For over 20 years, he had accumulated substantial expertise and experience in the areas listed above as well as land management, spatial information systems (GIS), policy analysis and advising, strategic planning, community development, urban development, slum upgrading, social and environmental sciences, and research techniques. Before joining UN-Habitat in 2007, Sietchiping worked for the Victoria State Government (Australia), the United Nations Economic Commission for Africa (UNECA), the private sector, University of the West Indies (Jamaica), University of Melbourne and Deakin University (Australia), University of Yaoundé (Cameroon) and the Civil Society Organisation (Cameroon). He holds a PhD in geography from the University of Melbourne (Australia).

Martino Stierli

Martino Stierli is The Philip Johnson Chief Curator of Architecture and Design at the Museum of Modern Art, where he oversees the wide-ranging programme of special exhibitions, installations and acquisitions of the Department of Architecture and Design. Stierli is the author of *Montage and the Metropolis: Architecture, Modernity and the Representation of Space* (Yale University Press, 2018) and *Las Vegas in the Rearview Mirror: The City in Theory, Photography, and Film* (Getty Research Institute, 2013). He has organised various exhibitions, including the international travelling exhibition *Las Vegas Studio: Images from the Archives of Robert Venturi and Denise Scott Brown*. At MoMA, he has curated, with Vladimir Kulić, the exhibition *Toward a Concrete Utopia: Architecture in Yugoslavia, 1948-1980*. Together with the other chief curators, he was responsible for the reconceptualisation of the collection installations in the newly expanded MoMA. He is currently working on an exhibition on modern architecture in South Asia in the post-independence period, and on contemporary Chinese architecture. Prior to joining MoMA, Martino was the Swiss National Science Foundation Professor at the University of Zurich's Institute of Art History. He has also taught at Columbia University and Princeton University, as well as at the universities of Zurich, Basel and ETH Zurich, from where he holds a PhD. His scholarship has been awarded numerous prizes and grants, most recently the 2019 Richard Schlagman Art Book Award (for *Toward a Concrete Utopia*).

Wang Jun

Wang Jun is Secretary of the CPC Songyang County Committee, Songyang County, China. He is responsible for the conceptualisation and implementation of strategies for regional revitalisation and the sustainable development of traditional villages. Through his efforts, a group of dying traditional villages in Songyang County were revitalised. Now, the State Ministry of Housing and Construction has named Songyang an exemplary county for the protection and development of traditional villages in China and the county ranks second in the Traditional Chinese Villages Catalogue. Songyang has also been chosen by the State Administration of Cultural Relics as a national experimental area for the protection of traditional villages, and by the China Heritage Conservation Foundation as the only pilot county in the country for the project "Action for Saving the Old Houses". The concept and practice of village revitalisation, as advocated by Wang Jun, initially explored the realisation of the ecological potentials of villages and has since become a national model and pioneer by raising awareness for value recognition and village protection, with positive impacts not only in China but also abroad. In 2016, Wang Jun was named one of the top ten "outstanding figures of traditional village guardians" in China.

Xu Tiantian

Xu Tiantian is the founding principal of DnA_Design and Architecture. She has received numerous awards such as the WA China Architecture Award in 2006 and 2008, the Architectural League New York's Young Architects Award in 2008, *Architectural Record*'s Design Vanguard Award in 2009 and the Moira Gemmill Prize for Emerging Architecture in 2019. She has built a number of projects, such as Songzhuang Art Center and Ordos Art Museum. In the past years she has been engaged extensively in the rural revitalising process in Songyang and Zhejiang Province. Her groundbreaking "architectural acupuncture" is a holistic approach to the social and economic revitalisation of rural China and has been selected by UN-Habitat as the case study of Inspiring Practice on Urban–Rural Linkages. Xu Tiantian received her masters degree in Architecture and Urban Design from Harvard Graduate School of Design, and her baccalaureate in architecture from Tsinghua University in Beijing.

Imprint

The Songyang Story

Architectural Acupuncture as Driver for Rural Revitalisation in China
Projects by Xu Tiantian, DnA_Beijing

Concept: Kristin Feireiss and Hans-Jürgen Commerell, Aedes Architecture Forum, Berlin
Project Management: Christine Meierhofer, Aedes Architecture Forum, Berlin
Design: Matthias Hübner, Berlin
Copy editor: Sophie Lovell, Berlin
Typefaces: Marfa by Dinamo & Alpina by Grilli Type
Pre-press, printing and binding: Graphicom, Vicenza

Park Books
Niederdorfstrasse 54
8001 Zurich
Switzerland
www.park-books.com

Park Books is being supported by the Federal Office of Culture
with a general subsidy for the years 2016–2020.

ISBN 978-3-03860-186-9